FELICETTE
The Space Cat

Stuart Atkinson

Published in 2023 by Stuart Atkinson

© Copyright Stuart Atkinson

Paperback version
ISBN: 9798859884452

Cover and Book interior setup by Russell Holden
www.pixeltweakspublications.com

Pixel Tweaks Publications
SELF PUBLISHING MADE SIMPLE

A Catalogue record for this book is
available from the British Library.

This book is dedicated to:

STELLA COXON,
my amazing partner, who supports
my writing so much...

CHI CHI PEGGY and JESS,
the cats we have shared together.

MY MUM,
who would have loved to have seen this book...

And finally...

FELICETTE herself.
I'm so, so sorry what they did to you.

CONTENTS

FOREWORD

I feel I should start with two warnings: Firstly, this is not a typical, fact-packed reference book about "space". It is the story of a cat. Secondly, it's a story without a happy ending.

This book is not full of tables and charts (did I just hear cheering?). Inside you'll find none of the usual photos of space boffins in crisp white shirts, standing in front of blackboards twiddling with clackety slide rules. There are no faded engineering blueprints, no space-walking astronauts waving at the camera with Earth shining blue and white far below them, nothing like that. If you're looking for an in-depth analysis of the state of space exploration in the early years of the 1960, with graphs showing expenditure vs profit etc, this isn't it.

This is simply the story of a cat called Félicette, "The Space Cat" as she's commonly referred to. Her life changed when she was dropped without warning into the high-tech 1960s Space Race world of rockets, engineers and new technology. She flew into space and returned, safely. If you're thinking "Never heard of her!" that's ok. Very few people know anything about her – and until a couple of years ago, neither did I. It's why I've written this book.

I first met Félicette when I was gathering material for a lecture about Laika, the first dog – indeed, the first animal - to go into orbit around Earth. At first I was just curious – what? A cat flew into space? Really? - but that curiosity soon turned to fascination and then to anger as I learned more and more about her and what had happened to her. The more I learned the clearer it became to me how wrong it was that while hundreds of millions of people know Laika's name and story, very few know anything about Félicette, or even knew that she existed. It was as if she'd been white-washed from history.

Then one particular image of Félicette - that I'll talk about later - appeared on my screen and as I felt my eyes swimming with tears I made her a promise that I would do everything I could to get her story "out there" into the world. This book is one way I'm keeping that promise.

I'm not the only person with that goal. Three days before I started writing this book a small bronze statue of Félicette was unveiled at a ceremony in Strasbourg, at the campus of the International Space University. That statue was only there because of the efforts of one man, another cat lover who felt Félicette had been ignored for too long. In 2017 Matthew Serge Guy mounted an online campaign to raise the funds needed to build a statue of Félicette, celebrating her short life and acknowledging her contribution to science, and it was successful. Sadly, but unsurprisingly, the ceremony wasn't shown on any of the TV news programmes I watch, and it hasn't appeared in any newspapers either. There was no fanfare, no fuss. It was as if it hadn't even happened.

I have tried to publish this book the traditional way – I've queried it with multiple agents and approached multiple publishers too, but no-one has shown any interest, perhaps understandable considering some aspects of the story – so I have decided to self-publish it. That means no fanfare or fuss, no big book launch, no huge publicity campaign… but that's ok. All I want to do is to bring Félicette's story out of the shadows and into the open, and this is my way of doing it. And now you're reading it, so thank you!

And now, having started with warnings, a confession: I'm an animal lover, always have been, always will be - but I haven't always been a cat person. For the first 40 years of my life I grew up around dogs and *only* dogs, without a cat in sight. I grew up playing with and walking an unbroken succession of mad labradors, elegant collies and wise retrievers, so it came as quite a shock to my system when, after moving to Kendal more than 15 years ago, my partner's very quiet and wise old white cat took a shine to me. It was an even greater but delightful and humbling shock when Chi Chi and I became inseparable best buddies, and my heart cracked straight down the middle when, 19 years old, she died, in my arms, on a vet's table after becoming just too ill and too tired to go on.

Two cats later I now find myself owned heart and soul by a criminally-pretty black and white rescue cat called Jess. When we brought her back from the sanctuary Jess spent the next three months hating me with a passion, glaring at me with all the warmth of Greta Thundberg watching Donald Trump buying an airplane ticket whilst eating a Big Mac. Now when I get back from work she greets me at the door as if she hasn't seen me for years and melts across my lap like a Salvador Dali clock as soon as I sit down.

I haven't turned my back on dogs though. I still pet them in the street, and until they both sadly passed away last year I used to end up on my mum's living room floor wrestling with her huge golden Labrador in a tangle of feet and paws... but one of my joys in life now is to lay down on my sofa and have Jess stretch out to her full length along my legs, looking like a cat draught excluder, or to have her curled up tightly into a ball on my lap so small I could almost hold her in one cupped hand. I look at her lying there and feel awe that such a tiny, gentle creature can hold so much love, and give it to me. I feel a lava-hot rage that so many people hurt animals like her for pleasure - or, perhaps worse, without feeling anything at all. And I feel driven to tell more people about Félicette.

So, this book is very different to the dozen books I've written and had published before. They have all been astronomy and science reference books, written for children, so when talking about "animal astronauts" I've had to reign myself in and just stick to cold, hard facts, skip over their fates and keep my personal feelings out of the writing. But this book is different. I haven't held back here. I haven't sugar-coated or white-washed anything. This is my very personal account of Félicette's story. You'll be able to tell that I wasn't happy when I wrote it. Some will think it's too harsh in places, too judgemental. Whatever. I'll live with their disapproval. This is the story that needs to be told – the true story, not a sterilised, offend no-one Disney screenplay.

So, if you're one of those people who hears a sad story involving an animal and shrugs it off with a huffy, dismissive "Oh, it's only a dog/cat/donkey/whatever!" then this book probably isn't for you. But if, like me, you believe we should treat animals with the respect they deserve, then it definitely is.

Right. Enough blathering. Here's Félicette's story. You won't have heard it before, but I promise you you'll never forget it.

Stuart Atkinson
Kendal
April 2022

INTRODUCTION

Years before humans dared to leave Earth others were sent into the unknown in their place. Animals, not people, were the first to reach, and break through, the final frontier.

Everyone interested in space knows the story of gentle Laika, the first dog to travel into – and tragically die in – Earth orbit, in 1957, sacrificed to make Yuri Gagarin's history-making flight possible four years later. Some even know how, in the same year, a grinning American chimpanzee called Ham gazed down on Earth's blue oceans and snow-white clouds from above, months before human astronauts Alan Shepherd and John Glen enjoyed the same magical view.

But these are just the most famous "animal astronauts". Many others have flown into space over the years. During the 50th anniversary of Apollo 11's historic landing on the Moon, many TV documentaries and films were released to celebrate it, including the story of how the brave crew of Apollo 8 were the first human beings to reach and orbit the Moon. However, none of them told their viewers that those astronauts were not the *first* of Earth's children to reach and orbit the Moon. Three months earlier, the Russian 'Zond 5' capsule rounded Earth's satellite, carrying some strange passengers: the first living beings to see Earthrise from the Moon were not square-jawed Apollo astronauts Frank Borman, Jim Lovell and Bill Anders, but a pair of rather bewildered tortoises – and to this day *no-one knows their names...*

In July 1959, two years after Laika's flight and a whole decade before Neil Armstrong took his "One small step", a veritable Space Ark was launched by the Russians. A capsule carrying two dogs and the first rabbit in space – "Marfusha" or "Little Martha" – blasted off, returning to Earth several days later. All its brave animal crew survived.

This book is the story of another "animal astronaut" hardly anyone has heard of: Félicette, the first **cat** to journey into space.

There's no happy ending, I'm afraid. But, just as Laika's story has been told many times, Félicette's story deserves to be told too. We owe her that.

ONE

FÉLICETTE – THE BEGINNING

If you research the story of Félicette online you'll find that her origins are shrouded in mystery and more than a little confusion. Many websites and blogs say she was a stray cat, plucked off the streets of Paris, but that's not the case. Laika – the first living creature to orbit the Earth - was a stray, certainly, but Félicette was not. In fact, Félicette was obtained, along with 13 other cats, from a "pet dealer".

Which one? No-one knows. Where were they? Again, unknown.

Obtained... Now what does *that* mean? *How* were they obtained? That's just the first of many mysteries that make up Félicette's fascinating story...

Let's be honest here. Considering the large number of cats involved, it's likely that it was all arranged very formally and officially. Presumably a Parisian cat dealer was contacted by post or over the phone and asked if they could supply a large number of cats for use in a scientific project and they did so in a cold, efficient business transaction. Occam's Razor suggests that some time later the cats were duly delivered in and unloaded from an unremarkable van in equally unremarkable boxes or crates. That makes perfect, if dull, sense.

But that scenario still poses intriguing question about the dealer. Where did *they* get the cats from? Did they have breeders supplying them with cats, or did they drive around Paris scooping cats up off the streets like the Child Catcher from Chitty Chitty Bang Bang until they'd filled their order? If so, Félicette might not have been a stray after all…

If Pixar, Disney or Spielberg ever make a film of Félicette's story, I'm sure her origins will be shown with more than a hint of artistic licence. I imagine it would be something like this. After the opening title fanfare and credits the music fades and the screen fills with an aerial shot looking down on an un-named street somewhere in Paris. As a caption tells the viewers it's a summer's day in early August 1963, the camera swoops down towards the ground, aiming for a single unremarkable door, the door to an unidentified shop. Standing outside the door is a tall man, looking very serious in a dark suit, with an even more serious expression on his face. He pushes on the door and it swings open with the sound of a tinkling bell, and as he steps inside we see the shop is a *pet* shop, crammed full of toys, feed, boxes, everything a loving pet owner could want. But the man strides past all this clutter, ignoring it, and all the other customers browsing too as he heads purposefully towards the back of the shop, clearly on a mission. As he pushes through a door at the rear of the shop he is met by a nervous-looking young woman who points towards a large cage on the floor. Inside are more than a dozen cats, some wrestling in a tangle of legs and tails, some skipping about or playing with toys, a few sitting on their own, including one small black and white cat that seems to be the outsider in the group. The man walks across to the cage and examines its contents. Anyone else would smile, or laugh, amused by the antics of the cats, but he just looks down, and nods. "Perfect," he says coldly, "I'll take them." *How many?* asks the young woman nervously. The man looks at her with a cool disregard. "*All* of them..."

Well, that's how I'd film it anyway...

But however they were "obtained", the first obvious question is: **why cats?**

Six years earlier a Russian dog called Laika had flown into space, and had become a global superstar as she orbited the Earth, travelling where no dog had gone before. Not that pretty, sweet-natured Laika had a chance to enjoy her fame; her mission had always been designed to be strictly one-way and she had died in space – horribly, it was only revealed many years later – seven hours or so into her flight, after just four orbits of the Earth. Her lifeless body then remained orbiting our planet inside Sputnik 2 for another five months before it burned up as a shooting star in Earth's atmosphere.

After Laika more dogs had flown into orbit, and other animals too, and soon many countries, not just the duel-ling post-war Superpowers, decided they needed to be "in space", for reasons of security, technological progress and, of course, national pride. The French were no exception, and they decided they needed to claim a lane in the Space Race. But instead of using dogs, or chimpanzees, they went with a rather smaller animal.

But not a cat.

On February 22nd 1961 France became the third country to send an animal into space when they launched a **rat** called Hector into space. Nine months later two more unnamed rats followed in Hector's paw-steps – but there's only so much you can learn from something as small as a rat. For the French, it was time to up their game. But rather than launching yapping dogs or gibbering chimpanzees into space as the Russians and Americans respectively had already done, the French space authorities decided, with typical French contrariness, to use cats.

Why? Officially the reason was that French scientists had already accumulated a lot of data about the neurology of (translation: they had *experimented on*) cats, so were well placed to be able to see how a cat would be affected by going into space. Maybe they were also drawn to cats for practical reasons – because they were smaller than dogs and so would need a smaller capsule. Maybe they thought cats, being famously independent, were more suited to flying in space on their own in a confined space. Or maybe it was because cats were and are still thought of as much more intelligent, elegant and sophisticated than dogs (and certainly grinning chimpanzees!) and so were somehow seen as more... *French.*

Whatever the reason, the decision was taken to send a cat into space onboard a French rocket, and the authorities started to plan the historic mission. Six years earlier Laika had been sent into space on a very ambitious mission which would see her orbiting the Earth several times over many hours. The first space cat's mission would be much less ambitious: they would go on a *sub-orbital* flight, basically rocketing straight up into space before coming down again only a handful of minutes later.

And there was another huge difference too. The scientists who sent Laika into space had packed her into her Sputnik 2 capsule knowing full well they were sending her to her death. The spacecraft had been built without any of the systems needed to return it, and its occupant, safely to Earth, so Laika was always going to die in space, one way or another. She was under a death sentence from the moment she was chosen.

But the first space cat's mission would end with it returning to Earth safely, after its capsule was jettisoned from its rocket and descended on parachutes. Once the capsule was located on the ground it would then be recovered and its feline occupant carefully retrieved from inside, hopefully still very much alive.

Although this mission profile was nowhere near as complicated as Laika's orbital mission it was still very challenging. If they could do all that, the French space scientists thought, they would gain priceless information about the effects of space travel on living creatures, information which would bring forward the glorious day a French astronaut followed Gagarin into orbit.

But first they needed a cat.

However they were "obtained" and however they arrived at the space centre, 14 felines – all of them female - were eventually delivered to the space scientists and the selection process began in earnest. It's easy to imagine all those white-shirted men standing in front of the cats, peering down at them, looking at them closely as they tumbled about excitedly, pulling on each other's ears and pushing their claws and noses through the bars of the cage they were held in.

We know that at this stage none of the cats had names. They came from the mysterious dealer without names, of course, and after arriving at the space centre were given identities consisting only of numbers and letters- a deliberate attempt to stop the scientists and others who would handle them becoming too attached to them.

We also know, thanks to photos taken later during their training, that there were cats of all different shapes and breeds in the group of "flight candidates". Those grainy pictures show a selection of brown and whites, tabbies, black and whites, all kinds of cats. Looking at the line up there are two jet black cats, both of which would have looked very much at home keeping a cackling witch company in her cottage in the woods. Another is a very pretty, delicate-looking ginger and white cat with huge, orb-like eyes, apparently quite a lot younger than the rest. Yet another is an older, big bruiser of a girl, her broad white face dabbed with two very distinctive black patches, one on her chin and the other on her nose, standing out starkly, like birthmarks. One other striking member of the group appears to have a lone black splodge just above her top lip, making comparisons with Hitler unfortunate but inevitable.

And there, always on the end of the line in every photo, is a small, black and white tuxedo cat, probably the smallest of the whole group. Two months after those group photos were taken, this little cat would make history and be given a proper name - Félicette. But during her training and flight she was known only as "C341".

On some of those photos C341's eyes are narrow slits, as she looks with suspicion at the strange new world she has found itself in. On other photos the cat's eyes are wide, either with alarm or fear, it's impossible to tell. There's no way of knowing because on all but a handful of the photos all that is visible of C341 – and of any of the cats – is her face.

Or rather, her *head*.

And this, I think, is one reason why Félicette's story is not as widely known as Laika's.

Do a Google image search for "Laika" and you will be rewarded with page after page of photos showing her looking happy and almost carefree. I've actually done just that to help me write this chapter. Here she is pictured standing on a table; there she is being held by one of her handlers, or standing up in her capsule; further down the page she is shown wearing her harness and being petted by someone. On every photo she actually looks excited to be where she is, and you can almost see her tail wagging and hear her yipping happily as she is prepared for her date with destiny. And on so many of the photos we can see *all* of her.

Not so the French "space cats". A similar Google image search for photographs of them will fill your screen with images that are very… different.

To appreciate *how* different we need to go back in time to the heady early days of the US space program, when the triumphant landing of Apollo 11 was many years away and Flying In Space was actually still the stuff of science fiction. In the early 1960s, at the same time the space cats were being chosen, the US test pilots and naval aviators who had passed their gruelling and invasive training to qualify to become astronauts were revealed to the world during high profile press conferences.

Those Mercury and Gemini astronaut candidates were led out like Love Island contestants and seated behind a long desk, dressed in sharp suits, their square jaws jutting out, #1 haircut stubble on their heads, grinning, laughing and joking with the press, swapping Alpha Male banter with each other, basking in the attention, happy to be there.

The most common images of the "space cats" shows them all lined up on display too, but unlike Alan Shepherd and John Glenn they are clearly *not* happy to be there.

Unlike Laika they are not seen standing up, tails wagging, ears pricked, looking wide-eyed at the world around them. All we can see of them are their heads, sticking out of what look like small white, wooden or metallic bird boxes, lined up on a shelf like ornaments. They look like they have been thrown into medieval stocks as some kind of punishment. It's obvious they can't move inside their boxes, not even a little, and anyone who knows how restless cats can get if held still for even a few moments looks at those photos and realises how utterly miserable they must have been.

To make matters worse, the photos show the cats have what appear to be large Lego bricks sticking out of their heads. These are actually packages of electrodes, surgically implanted into their brains to monitor their neurological activity during their flight. They are ugly things, abominations really, and many – myself included – believe that they are the reason why the story of the "space cat" is known by so few people: newspaper editors, magazine editors and other media outlets were understandably reluctant to use photos showing cute pussy cats apparently transformed into Frankenstein monsters by heartless space boffins.

So, where Laika looks like a normal dog on her photos, albeit a normal dog in a very unusual place, the French space cats have been reduced to disembodied heads, like something from a science fiction or horror film. It's as if their bodies don't exist, and all the scientists are interested in is the half pound or so of pale pink blancmange hidden inside their skulls.

If you go onto the popular online video sharing website YouTube you can find a nine-minute long film with footage of Félicette being prepared for her flight. It's not an easy watch, so if you're not sure you can handle it don't go looking for it. But if you want the complete story it's something you need to see. I personally find it deeply disturbing in many places, and I'll be referring back to it many times over the next few chapters, so it might be a good idea to stop reading here and go check it out, but beware: one of its most disturbing sequences shows a scientist inserting a lead into the electrode block embedded in one of the space cats' heads. It's not done gently, or delicately; it's done with all the love and consideration of someone impatiently plugging a SCART lead into the back of their TV.

I said earlier how none of the cats had been given names, to prevent the scientists from becoming close to or find of them. Actually, one *was* given a name, and ironically it was because of those awful electrodes.

While 13 of the cats seemed to have had no adverse reactions to their electrodes, one did, and her health began to deteriorate. To give the mission scientists credit where it's due, rather than just rejecting the ailing cat and putting her down they removed the electrodes and made the cat the mission mascot, giving her the nickname "Scoubidou" after a scoubidou bracelet they found around her neck.

If you're wondering what one of those was – and I had to check - the bracelets were nothing to do with the cowardly, snack-munching, crime-solving dog Scooby-Doo; that hugely-popular cartoon series didn't air until many years later, in

1969 in fact, so there was no connection or link between the two animals.

No, a scoubidou was a type of braided, weaved friendship bracelet-type thing, very popular at the time, especially with children. They even featured in a very popular song sung by suave French singer Sacha Distel –

Hang on a minute…

If the cat was found wearing a bracelet around its neck, doesn't that suggest it had belonged to someone? Unless it was incredibly clever and made it itself, then somehow slipped it over its own neck to show off to its non-weaving friends, it had that scoubidou put on it by someone, suggesting it was owned by someone, as a pet, doesn't it? So we're taken back to the rather awkward question of how the dealer who supplied the cats to the space agency obtained them in the first place. Maybe the "dealer" *had* rounded up street cats instead of taking them from a breeder? And maybe Félicette *was* a "street cat" after all?

We'll never know. However the space cats were obtained, Scoubidou had a very lucky escape, thanks to the electrodes that had been fitted to – and rejected – by her skull.

The images taken of the cats fitted with their electrodes are jarring and upsetting, and although we can comfort ourselves with the knowledge that we'd never do that sort of thing today, that it was "a different time" and that "times have changed" when I look at those photos of the cats lined up in their boxes I can't help wondering how scared and confused they were as cameras clicked and flashbulbs popped around them.

And there on those photos, on the end of the line, is C341, a small, black and white tuxedo cat, staring out from her prison cell box with angry, narrowed eyes, wondering what the hell is going on. Two months later she would be christened Felix by the French media, and then re-christened more appropriately *Félicette*. But more on that later.

Before she had been "obtained" from the dealer by the space agency, Félicette had been just another cat destined to be bought by someone and taken away to a new life as their family pet. If things had turned out differently, if fate had taken a different turn, she could have ended up in some family home somewhere, living out her nine lives there with a bed beside a crackling fire to curl up and sleep in, food and water freely available, shiny and noisy toys to play with on the carpet and several welcoming laps to choose from when she grew tired. But that life – the life all cats deserve - was stolen from her.

Or was it? Let's be honest here. Not all cats go to good homes. Perhaps if she hadn't been taken by that dealer to the space agency that little Tuxedo cat would have gone to a dark place *without* love and affection; to a place with a cold, bare floor for a bed, scraps of food to live on and no soft laps to curl up on. She might even have been *disposed of* after a few months if no-one bought her. Maybe she had a lucky escape?

We'll never know, because fate had other plans for C341. She was destined to go further and higher than any cat had before, and to this day no cat has gone any further or higher than she did in October 1963.

But first, like all astronaut candidates, C341 had to pass her training…

TWO

TRAINING

Going into space isn't like jumping in the car to go on a shopping trip in town, or getting onto a bus and travelling across the country to visit a long-distance partner at university. You have to prepare both your body and mind; you have to train them to be strong enough for the stresses and strains of a journey that is as unnatural as it is dangerous. If you skipped that part, if you did no training at all before blast-off you'd be totally unprepared for the deafening sounds, bone-shaking violence and cheek-wobbling acceleration you'd experience during the flight. Within minutes you'd be a gibbering, sobbing wreck, driven half mad by it all.

Now imagine how a *cat* – an animal used to roaming freely, used to hunting and stalking out in the open, used to being independent, used to doing what it wanted to do when it wanted to - would react to suddenly being strapped without warning or preparation into a strait jacket, bolted into an enclosed capsule and fired into space. They'd go absolutely crazy, or die of fear, or both.

Which is why the French space cats, just like their grinning human counterparts, were put into a "training programme".

But how do you train a cat to go into space?

If you're a cat owner you probably laughed out-loud just reading that sentence, because the very idea of trying to *train* a cat to do *anything* is ridiculous. Now a *dog*, yes. *They* can be trained. They actually get joy out of being trained to fetch things – balls, sticks, slippers, papers, etc. It doesn't matter what it is they'll happily lollop after it, bring it back and drop it at your feet, over and over, certain they're playing The Best Game Ever. More practically, dogs can be trained to come when you call them, to walk at your heel, to roll over and play dead. They can be trained to round up sheep and guide them into pens. They can be trained to rescue earthquake survivors, detect drugs and guide blind people. Why? Because dogs *want* to please their owners; they have a need, deep in their doggy DNA, to serve us and be rewarded and appreciated for it.

Cats, on the other hand, don't care if they please you or not. Cats will hear you calling their name and totally ignore you. Why? Because cats don't feel any need to serve. In fact the very idea of serving is alien to them. Cats are above all that. Cats think – no, they *know* – they are better than us, that it's *our* duty to serve *them*, so they don't do the "fetch" thing. It's beneath them. Oh, they'll play with you alright, scamper across the room in pursuit of a thrown piece of scrunched up paper or an over-priced catnip toy with a cheap bell inside it, and then body slam it and claw it at it with their hind legs like a Jurassic Park raptor taking down a fat tourist, but only when they *want* to; it's not for *your* pleasure. And when they're bored with playing they will just stop, turn on their heels and walk off regally, without even looking at you over their shoulder.

Train a cat?

Yeah. Right.

So, looking back at the "training" of those space cats you have to ask *who did they think they were kidding?* They might have convinced themselves that they were training the cats to prepare for their flights, making them stronger and more able to deal with the launch, re-entry and landing, but all they were doing really was finding out which ones were the least terrified by and the most tolerant of their methods and machines. Nothing could have prepared those animals for the violence and fury of going into space. *Nothing.* But a training programme was devised, and the space cats were thrown into it.

We've all seen footage of human astronauts training, on TV shows and in films. During the recent 50th anniversary of the Apollo 11 Moon landing dozens of documentaries showed how the Apollo astronauts strapped onto beds and into chairs, covered with sensor pads, hooked up to machines and studied like lab rats; how they were put into isolation chambers to test their mental strength and how they coped with being restricted and confined; how they were whirled and swirled and swooped and swooshed around and around and around in centrifuges to see how they would stand up to the high g-forces experienced during launch and landing. And those training methods haven't really changed. Half a century after the gold and silver Eagle landed at Tranquility Base, astronauts still have to undergo years and years of training before they fly up to the space station. They, and the astronauts who have their sights set on flying further - to the Moon and, one day, to Mars - are still human pin cushions, and still regularly thwump-whump around a track strapped inside a centrifuge, like James Bond in "Moonraker".

And although their equipment wasn't as high tech or expensive as the machines used today, the space cats trained in much the same way humans did then and do now.

But there was one huge difference. None of the Mercury, Gemini or Apollo had electrodes embedded in their brains.

Each space cat candidate was surgically fitted with a package of electronics designed to "assess their neurological activity" during the mission. That obscene Lego brick sticking out of the top of their heads is what looks so horrific in the photographs of Félicette.

That done, the cats' training could finally begin. And it would last for two months.

The space cats, including C341, were trained using several different pieces of equipment, some more stressful than others, but all of them undoubtedly stressful in some way.

They were put into small containers and fitted with constraining cloths and collars for long periods to test how badly they were affected by being confined. I can imagine how much they hated that, how much they hatred not being able to even move, let alone run away to safety. They were also placed in soundproof boxes and forced to endure simulations of the noises they would experience during blast off - the roar of the rocket engines, the clunking and clanking of the launch, etc. And you don't have to have a degree in veterinary science to imagine how traumatic that was for the cats; with their super sensitive hearing, cats can hear much better than us and much better even than dogs.

And, of course, they were put into a centrifuge and spun around and around and around to simulate the increased g forces of lift-off and re-entry. For C341 and her fellow candidates, the phrase "Not enough room to swing a cat" was not applicable.

Human trainee astronauts take their seats in a centrifuge knowing full well what is about to happen. As the straps are tightened across their chests and they wriggle down into their acceleration couches they take a deep breath and know in advance that when the bizarre contraption starts moving their bodies will feel heavier and heavier, their eyes will start to press back into their sockets and their breathing will become a struggle. They know that soon they'll be hearing a dull whumpf-whumpf-whumpf through the walls of their capsule as the centrifuge picks up speed and spins them faster and faster.

C341 and her fellow astronaut candidates would have had no idea in advance what was going to happen, and no idea what was happening as the centrifuge did its job. All they would have known was that suddenly, for some reason, they couldn't move, couldn't breathe and felt so, so heavy.

In that YouTube film I mentioned earlier there is a short sequence showing one of the cat candidates being spun around on a kind of pedestal contraption that looks more like a potter's wheel - or the "Spinning Cat" Craggy Island fairground attraction on Father Ted - than a piece of high-tech space machinery. It's not *the* centrifuge, just a smaller version of one, but even so the cat, locked up in a box, is clearly in distress and can be heard crying out plaintively as it is span round relatively slowly. This is followed by another sequence showing the main centrifuge whumping around at a much higher speed. It can't be seen but I can imagine how scared the cat inside it was.

During this initial training period the cats were also fitted into the constraining contraptions which would hold them in place inside the capsule during the flight.

Now, anyone who has ever had – or even just *known* – a cat will know that you can't just push one into a space, close the door behind it and expect it to sit down, cross its paws and relax; that doesn't work even for a cat being put into a carry box for a trip across the street to the vet. The scientists knew the cat would have to be restrained if they were to gather any useful data from its flight, so they built special containers that would hold the cat firmly in place inside the capsule. Once the cat was inside the container, and secured using a combination of straps and fittings so it couldn't move, the whole thing would then be slid sideways into the capsule, like a shell being loaded into a cannon.

Photographs of these "dollies" as they were called are not easy to look at. The cats inside them are basically immobilised, with no bodily movement possible. Their heads can move, just, as you can tell from the way the cats' faces are oriented in slightly different positions on different images; they can look left or right, a little, and up and down, a little. But that's it.

I've found quite a few photos showing C341 in her container, and in the vast majority she looks pretty placid – not happy by any means, not content, but she's not struggling or protesting. However, in one segment of the previously mentioned YouTube film she looks very different.

In it, Félicette is shown shrinking away from the person who is holding her and her container, off camera to her right. Her head is twisted around to the left and her eyes are wide open. Staring straight into the camera, she looks so sad, so vulnerable. I can almost hear her asking "Why are you doing this to me?"

And then she starts to meow and cry. It's very hard to watch.

But there is a still image I haven't been able to get out of my head since the first time it popped up in a Google image search. Out of all the many photographs and video clips I've found during my research for this book it is the most disturbing.

In this image, Félicette's container is sitting on a table or shelf of some kind, and we can see more of her body because the container's sides are absent. But in this photo, rather than looking placid, Félicette is clearly *fighting*. She has her head thrown back in anger and defiance. Her eyes are wide open, her mouth is open too, revealing her teeth and fangs. I look at that picture, at the look on her face, and I can almost hear her screaming "GET ME OUT OF THIS!!!!"

I *hate* that picture. If I had a TARDIS (other time machines are available) I'd set its controls for that very place at the very moment it was taken, fall back through time, throw open its doors, dash out, push aside the photographer and grab that container off its shelf. I'd undo every strap, every buckle until Félicette was free then gather her up in my arms and carry her into the TARDIS, slamming the doors shut behind me. Then I'd take her somewhere safe, somewhere where she could never be strapped into that space age iron maiden casket again. It was abuse. Nothing more, nothing less.

It was a different time... We wouldn't do that now... Perhaps. But we shouldn't have done it then.

How did the training go? I've not been able to find any detailed reports about that, but it must have helped the scientists decide some cats *were* more suitable flight candidates than others because at the end of those two months 6 out of the 13 remaining cats were chosen to go through to the next stage of the bizarre Space X Factor contest that they had been entered into against their will. They must have been chosen because they came through the various tests with the least negative reactions, and because the scientists thought they had the best chance of not just surviving the mission but contributing useful science to it by not freaking out in the capsule and ruining their measurements.

But more about that in the next chapter.

THREE

HARDWARE

It sounds obvious I know, but to go into space an astronaut – human or feline – needs a rocket.

By the beginning of October 1963 C341 and her companions had completed their initial training. All that remained was for one of them to be chosen for the dubious honour of becoming the first cat to fly into space. But that decision wouldn't be made where they had trained with their centrifuges and other equipment. It would be made many, many miles away, in Algeria, in the middle of the Saharan desert near the town of Hammaguir, at a remote launch site close to the equator at the Centre interarmees d'essais d'engins speciaux ("Interarmy Special Vehicles Test Centre") where the rocket that would soon take one of them into space was being prepared.

When I first saw a photo of the launch site taken at the time it looked naggingly familiar – a scattering of small, low buildings, surrounded by miles and miles of wide-open desert. Where had I seen it before? Then it hit me: it looks just like that "hive of scum and villainy" Mos Eisley Spaceport in the first Star Wars film.

Of course, no droids cheeped and chirped around the Hammaguir launch site, no Jawas skulked in its shadows and

and no levitating speeder cars raced around its streets either, but planes came and went, and at the start of October 1963 one ugly but very special plane dropped down towards the base and set down on its dusty landing strip. The distinctly unglamorous Bristol 170, a snub-nosed twin-propeller plane commonly used at the time for carrying cars and other bulky cargo across country in its unpressurised cabin, was carrying a small army of handlers, ground staff, engineers and technicians – and the space cats. After the plane had taxied to a halt the cats were unloaded off the plane and taken to cabins which would be their homes for the rest of their stay.

If those cabins had windows, perhaps C341 or one of her companions was able to look out of it and see their rocket being prepared out in the desert. We'll never know. But we do know what that rocket was like.

When Laika flew into space on November 3rd 1957 her capsule was carried by a Sputnik P5 rocket that was almost 30m tall, roughly the same height as the Vostok rocket that would carry Yuri Gagarin into space four years later, on April 12th 1961. The pencil-thin Redstone rocket that carried Alan Shepard, the first US astronaut into space inside his Mercury capsule a little less than a month later was slightly smaller at 25m high, but it didn't have enough power to put him into orbit. It did, however, look like a rocket should look.

In contrast, with its tail fins and sharp pointy nose the Veronique AGI rocket chosen to carry the first cat into space looked more like a James Bond villain's missile, or a child's drawing of a rocket. Indeed, compared to the mighty, snow white Saturn Vs which would eventually take astronauts to the Moon, the Veronique looked like and was little more than a firework. But it was good enough to do the job, and although it looked very… basic… it had some very clever

21

technology incorporated into it. For example, the rocket did not need a conventional launch tower to blast off from; four long, narrow horizontal fins, or struts, supported its weight on the launch pad, like the splayed legs of a Christmas tree stand.

Officially classed as a "sounding rocket", the Veronique rocket was designed to whoosh payloads up to the edge of space but not much further. It wasn't designed or built to launch satellites, and definitely not to carry a French Gagarin or Shepard. But it was powerful enough to carry a small cat, and as C341 and her companions were reaching the end of their training in France it was being prepared on its launch pad, 1000s of miles away, in dusty Algeria.

Its flight plan was quite simple. It would blast off then, after jettisoning its struts and after an engine burn of 42 seconds, it – and the cat inside the capsule inside its nose cone - would reach a maximum altitude of 152 km before being pulled back down to the Earth again by gravity. After re-entry the capsule would deploy parachutes to brake its fall, and land around 13 minutes after it taken off, to be retrieved by a ground team.

At least, that was the plan.

However, as has so often been the case with rockets through the ages, as engineers and technicians prepared the rocket and its systems for flight things didn't go as planned. When its heading beacon was tested inside a helicopter it didn't work and had to be fixed. Then there were problems receiving data from the instruments packed into the rocket's nose cone. Then the homing beacon – which would help ground crews to locate the capsule after it had landed – wouldn't work. Eventually all these issues and other gremlins were sorted out, and by October 16th the rocket was ready to fly.

The next day, October 17th, was D Day for the space cats. With the Veronique rocket signed off as ready to go, with all the instruments checked and working, with all the ground crew ready to do their jobs, it was time for the mission scientists to select the 6 best-qualified of the space cat candidates to go through to the next stage – a last day of tests and discussions before the very final decision was made and one of them was selected to be the first cat to go into space.

What were they looking for at this late stage? It's hard to say. Certainly they would have made their choice based on how well the cats had responded to their training – i.e. how much they had been upset or disturbed by the simulated noises and g-forces they experienced – but they were looking for a cat with a good general demeanour too, a quiet cat that wouldn't give them any trouble.

By the end of the day a decision had been made: the quiet little black and white tuxedo cat, C341, would be the feline Yuri Gagarin. Fatefully, one thing that swung the decision in her favour was that she was the only cat that was the required weight; all the other cats had managed to put *on* weight during their training…

So C341 was chosen to become the first cat to fly into space, and another cat – unnamed - was chosen as her back-up, in case of any last-minute problems.

The die was cast. The next day, October 18th 1963, history would be made.

One way or another.

FOUR

A CAT IN SPACE

October 18th 1963. The Big Day. The day the first cat would fly into space. And after two months of being tested, experimented and operated on in a bizarre, disturbing combination of the X Factor, The Hunger Games and The Island of Dr Moreau, a quiet little black and white tuxedo cat known only as "C341" had been chosen to go down in history.

It was time for her for flight.

By now C341 looked very different than she had the day before. She already had those electrodes in her skull, remember, but it turned out they were only the start. After being selected as the prime candidate for the mission, C341 was fitted with even more sensors so her condition could be monitored during her flight. To complement a microphone fitted to the nose cone of the Veronique rocket, another microphone was attached to her chest to allow the teams on the ground to monitor her breathing. More electrodes were fitted to her front left leg and her right back leg to monitor her cardiac activity during her flight. Finally, another pair of electrodes was fitted to an unidentified "foreleg" (I'm thinking probably her right one, seeing as the left one already had the cardiac electrodes on it?) which would provide C341 with "stimulation" using "electrical impulses" during her flight.

Yes, that's right. Having already embedded electrodes in her brain, they fitted the cat with equipment which would actually give her electric shocks during her mission.

Now fitted with all her flight sensors, C341 had to be put into her capsule. First she was lifted up and placed in her sled-like dolly. Then she was strapped in tightly, so she couldn't move, and then finally, after all her various connections had been hooked up like a home cinema surround sound system, the dolly with her inside it was slid into a round housing in the nose cone of the rocket.

I'm not sure of the precise timeline of all this; it's not very clear from the YouTube video. The video shows it is still dark at the launch site, and the pad crew are working by the light of floodlights mounted on the support gantry, so C341 must have been put into the Veronique rocket – now standing vertically after being towed out to its launch site horizontally - sometime in the early hours of October 18th, What isn't clear is *when* she was put *into* that dolly. Was she taken to the launch site already crammed into it, or was she not put into until the last possible moment? I hope the latter, if only so she could have enjoyed a little more freedom, but I'm very doubtful; the YouTube film shows her inside the dolly, being held up by someone and shown to the camera, in fact that's the sequence I mentioned before which shows her pushing away from the person holding her, and shows her bleating helplessly too.

Maybe she sensed what was coming next.

Whatever the exact timeline of events was, some time before the Sun rose on October 18th, 1963, C341 was hooked up to all her monitoring systems and slid into the rocket head-first, like a bullet being loaded into a gun. The round metal plate at the rear of her dolly was screwed firmly into place with four screws, and that was that. She was onboard, sealed inside. Now the engineers and technicians ran yet more tests and checks to make absolutely sure that they could monitor C341 during her flight. Once they were satisfied that everything was ok they approved the flight.

The clock was now well and truly ticking.

But how long did it tick *for?*

Not many people know that poor Laika had been stuck in her Sputnik 2 capsule for a long time before she actually launched. Three days she sat in her capsule on top of that rocket; three long, perishingly-cold *days*. Kindly technicians rigged up a makeshift heater to provide Laika with some warmth by pumping hot air into her capsule through a snaking hose attached to a small heater, but still, she must have been very cold and uncomfortable. Thankfully, C341 didn't get put through that torture; I think there must only have been a matter of a few hours between her insertion into the capsule inside her dolly and the blast off of the rocket, because using one of the astronomy apps on my phone I've worked out that sunrise at the launch site on October 18th 1963 occurred at approx. 07.30, just as a bloated, big Full Moon was setting in the west. The Veronique rocket blast off time is recorded as 08:09, just over half an hour later, so I'm *hoping* that means Félicette wasn't kept lingering inside her cramped capsule for too long after being put into it.

So, as the Sun came up over the Saharan desert on the morning of October 18th, C341 was in her rocket. The siege engine-like service tower structure cocooning the rocket was removed, moved away by hand by pad rats manually turning and cranking handles to roll it away on rail tracks, leaving the

Veronique exposed, standing freely on its launch platform, a sleek needle pointed straight up at the pale blue morning sky. Now it was just a matter of waiting for everything to fall into place, for the very final checks to be made, and then the historic flight could begin.

While technicians and engineers scurried around on the ground beneath her, nervously checking screens, anxiously looking at readouts, carefully ticking off events from the pre-launch sequence timeline as they happened, C341 was lying down inside the tip of the rocket, unable to move, alone, and in absolute darkness. She could probably hear the hissing and clanking of the rocket coming up from far beneath her as it prepared for flight, but all she could do was lie there, prone, with her front legs stretched out before her, staring at the cold, bare metal wall of her capsule mere inches away from her nose.

I wonder how she felt as the time ticked away, totally unaware of what was happening to her and why it was happening. Was she just baffled by it all? Was she scared? I imagine she must have been; it's hard to think of a less natural environment for an animal that loves and needs its freedom.

I'm sure she wondered where everyone had gone. The YouTube film clearly shows the space cats had been surrounded by people ever since their training had begun - the various engineers, technicians and scientists all involved in the mission - so they hadn't been starved of human contact. Several sequences of the film show C341 and the other cats being stroked or petted by mission personnel as they are carried around in their boxes or positioned on a piece of apparatus, although to me it looks rather forced, like they had been ordered by the cameraman and their bosses to "play with the cat" or something like that to make it look less disturbing. But even so, C341 and her fellow flight candidates had been around people for the two months of their training and would have gotten used to them being there. Like all abductees – because that's what they were, really – they would have developed different relationships with different people, looked upon some more kindly than others. I'm sure they had their favourites, as all cats do.

I'm also very sure that some of the mission team became genuinely fond of the cats, despite that having been strongly discouraged. Remember, in a deliberate attempt to stop mission personnel becoming attached to them the cats they had just been given numbers, not actual names. But that won't have mattered; just as Scoubidou was given a nickname others would have been too, by some of the team anyway, just as they'll have been given sneaky ear scratches and nose rubs, even cuddles.

Suddenly all those people, the liked and disliked, the kind and the cold, were gone.

And what about the *other* cats? Cats are social creatures, they like being with other cats. Not all the time, no, but they will bond with other cats if placed into an environment with them. I'm sure C341 made "friends" with others in the group during their training, probably even became quite close to some of them during their brief time together. But suddenly they were gone too.

As the countdown began, C341 was lying in the dark, immobile and helpless. And totally and utterly alone.

At just after 08.00am local time the final "Go" decision was made to launch the Veronique rocket. It wasn't standing on the kind of traditional launch pad shown supporting

Saturn 5s, space shuttles and SpaceX rockets; there was no tall, skinned skyscraper of scaffolding, walkways and girders supporting it on one side. Betraying their V2 heritage, Veronique rockets launched from out in the open, more like large model rockets. So when the command to launch was given, at 08:09am, no leads or hoses were wrenched out of and swung away from it; no great slow motion bursts of orange fire or churning clouds of grey and white smoke billowed out of trenches dug beneath it. The Veronique just shot up into the sky like the glorified firework it was, riding on a long, fluttering flame. Moments later the quartet of support struts were jettisoned from the rocket's base, falling and tumbling away like sticks, and it continued up into the sky without them – but with C341 inside.

The Veronique's engines fired furiously for 49 seconds, pushing the little rocket skywards with such power that cocooned inside her capsule, up at the tip of the rocket, its cat passenger experienced acceleration forces of 9.5g. To put that rather meaningless figure into some context, the Moon-bound Apollo astronauts strapped into their mighty Saturn Vs, shaking and shuddering in their seats, experienced only 4g during launch. Their successors, riding onboard the rather more luxurious space shuttles, felt only *3g* as they headed into orbit. In 2008 the three crew members of the Expedition 16 mission to the International Space Station experienced a force of almost 8g as their Soyuz capsule plummeted to Earth off course. Two of the three were injured, with one requiring treatment in hospital for neck and back pain. So for a small cat to experience a chest-crushing 9.5g must have been an incredible strain, and terrifying too.

The Veronique rocket reached the highest point in its trajectory at an altitude of 152km or 94 miles. That's an important figure because it means that although they didn't go into orbit around the Earth, as Laika had done in Sputnik 2, the Veronique's capsule – and its passenger – officially made it into space by crossing the "Karman Line", the internationally agreed height of 100km at which "space" is said to begin.

If you're expecting to read here an uplifting section waxing lyrical about how C341 now experienced the joy and freedom of weightlessness, I'm sorry to have to disappoint you. Because she didn't.

In the movies you can always tell when a spaceship has reached that magical, mystical place called "space" because the stirring background music used during the launch suddenly dies (or is replaced by a cheesy angelic choir) and the people in the ship all stop talking and turn as one to look at something in the cabin that is suddenly rising up into the air – a pen, a flight manual, something like that. Then they see their own hands lifting up slowly, and they smile. Grinning, they unbuckle their clinking harnesses and then *they're* floating up out of their seats too, as if levitating, and as they drift upwards, arms and legs flailing, they grin at each other like kids locked overnight in a toyshop.

The message is clear: look at us, floating in zero gravity! We Are In SPAAAAAAAAAAACE..!!

Inside her capsule C341 experienced none of that. She was strapped into her dolly in the darkness so tightly there was no chance of her floating *anywhere*. She couldn't even move.

She must have *felt different* though. She must have felt her body *trying* to float out of its constraints; must have felt dizzy and disoriented as the fluids in her inner ears suddenly started behaving weirdly; must have felt the fluids covering her eyes becoming strangely sticky and wobbly. Maybe she felt space-sick, as many human astronauts do? We'll never know.

However she felt, C341 was "in space" for around five minutes. Then, with insufficient power to carry it on into orbit the rocket began to descend again.

Now it was time for the capsule to separate from the rocket in preparation for landing. It was jettisoned, and inside it C341 experienced "only" $\frac{1}{2}$/g for a while before, 8 minutes and 55 seconds after launch, the capsule's parachutes opened with a crack and it began to fall rather more slowly towards the ground, swinging and swaying beneath its fluffed-out canopies. Inside, the g forces on C341 lessened considerably too.

13 minutes after it had been blasted off the ground atop its Veronique rocket the capsule landed back down on the ground. It landed on its side, so C341 was left pitched forwards inside it in her dolly, with her head facing down and her bottom sticking up in the air. She must have been very uncomfortable while she hung upside down like that, waiting to be rescued from her confinement.

As the capsule's parachute fluttered down from the sky, crumpling onto the ground a short distance away, an antenna popped out of the base of the capsule and began transmitting a homing signal for a helicopter recovery team to follow.

Some time after that – and I've not been able to find out just how long – the recovery team spotted the capsule from their helicopter and landed nearby. When they reached the capsule they found it dented and dusty but intact, and quickly set about checking to see if its passenger had survived. The YouTube film shows the recovery team pulling C341's dolly out of the nose cone, like James Bond defusing a nuclear warhead, and the cat inside it has not only survived but is wide awake, alert, and *very* vocal. Clearly they are not at all impressed by what has just happened to them and what they've been put through -

But I'll be honest: I'm not sure the film actually shows Félicette. I'm wondering if it shows one of the other cats during a test of some kind.

The film on YouTube is so heavily edited it's not wise to take it any of it on face value or trust it too much. In some places the chronology of events seems a bit mixed up, and the same extreme close up face shot of C341 is used in several different places. And when I looked closely at the sequence showing C341 being retrieved from her capsule, I thought "Hang on... that's not her..."

The film is very grainy so it's hard to be sure, but when I watch that sequence a voice in my head tells me that the cat shown looks much more like a tabby than a black and white tuxedo. When I did some image processing work on a screenshot from the video the light and dark patterning on the cat's face doesn't look like the patterning on C341's...

Now, to be clear, I'm not suggesting the landing or any part of the mission was faked! But I am wondering if that much-viewed YouTube film isn't a 100% accurate record of the mission.

Regardless of what that film shows, there can be no doubt that back at the control centre at the launch sight everyone must have been delighted.

It looked like everything had worked perfectly! The launch had gone off without a hitch, the capsule had reached space and returned from it, landing safely on its parachutes, and its furry occupant had survived!

Back at the base the scientists were impatient to get to work. What had happened to C341 *during* her flight? What had all their sensors, electrodes and microphones learned?

It was time to bring C341 back to find out.

FIVE

AFTER THE MISSION

Exactly as planned, the multiple sensors attached to C341's legs had monitored her during the mission and sent back a stream of information. The electrodes embedded in her head did the same thing too. When the capsule was brought back to the launch site the techs and engineers there were anxious to get their hands on those recorders, and set about carefully removing them so they could be hooked up to readers and the data stored on them retrieved and studied.

So how had C341 fared during her brief but historic flight?

Very surprisingly, considering she had experienced a chest-crushing force of 9.5g after lift off, the results from the sensors showed that C341 had not been, quote, "adversely affected" during the blast off and ascent stages of the mission. She had been "alert" but had showed no obvious signs of stress. During the weightless phase of the flight she had actually been quite relaxed, and her "rhythms" (whatever that means) had all been slow. It was noted that her breathing had been very relaxed, suggesting she found this phase of her flight actually quite relaxing.

Cats, eh?

Unfortunately her return to Earth had been a lot *less* relaxing. The instruments' results showed she had experienced heart trouble as the capsule re-entered the atmosphere and plunged down through it, probably because it was spinning and vibrating so much as she experienced a force of over 7g.

The results of the instruments also showed that C341 had received "stimuli" – a polite term for the electric shocks they shot into her through those electrodes on her leg – more often than had been scheduled, and of a greater strength too. I have a lot of trouble with this aspect of the flight, I'll be honest. It was bad enough that they gave her electric shocks at all, but the fact they had given her more shocks and stronger shocks than originally planned is both shocking and very upsetting.

But, generally, the results showed that C341 had not been badly affected by her brief flight into space, which must have been a relief for any of the team members who had looked after her and bonded with her during their brief time together.

With the flight completed, the first scientific results collected, and C341 safely back on the ground – and, going by the YouTube video's timeline, happy enough after her flight to be able to tuck into her food again – it was time to let the world know about France's achievement. The media were given the results of the flight, and soon everyone knew C341's story.

And soon she had a name too.

When the French media ran the story, they were, understandably, very excited. It was a triumph for France, for its scientists and engineers! The fact that France had put a cat rather than a dog into space was a big deal, and soon C341's picture was on the front pages of French newspapers. And, inevitably, she was quickly given a nickname – *Felix*, after the mischievous black and white cartoon cat which was very popular at the time. Of course, that was totally wrong as C341 was female, so CERMA took the nickname and changed it to the feminine version.

Finally, after months of training when she was referred to only by her number, "space cat C341" had a proper name: "Félicette", pronounced "Fay-lee-set".

But what happened to Félicette *immediately after* that is something of a mystery.

According to all the records, reports and write ups I've been able to find, Félicette spent the two months after her mission "having more tests". Which tests? Unknown. Where? Also unknown, but surely she wouldn't have stayed at that launch site out in the middle of nowhere, she'd have been brought back to France, most likely Paris. Did she remain the property of the fledgeling space agency? Probably, considering what eventually happened to her – which I'll come to soon enough. Was she kept alone, in isolation, or was she allowed to rejoin the other space cats? The YouTube film shows a sequence where lots of cats are all giddily playing together after the flight, but I can't spot Félicette in that crazy crowd, and there's no way of knowing when that footage was taken anyway; the film is so disjointed it could have been taken at any time between the space cats arriving for their initial training and their assumed return to Paris. The truth is we just don't know what happened to Félicette during those two post-mission months.

But sadly we do know what happened to another one of her group.

On October 20th, just two days after Félicette's successful flight, another cat – again unnamed, but perhaps Félicette's "understudy" from her flight – was put into another dolly and slid into another Veronique, the aim being to launch the second cat into space as soon as possible, most likely in order to confirm the results gathered during Félicette's flight; scientists like repeating experiments so they can check and confirm their data.

But this second flight was doomed from the start.

First, an explosive bolt holding the rocket down malfunctioned during blast off, so instead of rising up cleanly and vertically into the sky the rocket shot off at a steep angle like a faulty firework, heading far out into the desert. The rocket didn't make it into space; it crashed into the desert some distance away from the launch site. To make matters worse the nose cone's transponder had failed on the launch pad, which made it very hard for the launch team to locate the crashed rocket. Eventually, after who knows how long, a helicopter spotted the parachute down on the ground, but in such a remote place they were unable to land there. After *another* delay ground vehicles were sent out to retrieve the rocket and its payload but when they eventually reached the crash site they were unable to get to the capsule because of some barbed wire. That caused yet more delay. Eventually, a whole day later, a second helicopter was sent out and this one did manage to land safely at the crash site.

But when its crew reached the wreckage they found that the rocket's nose cone was badly damaged, and the cat inside the capsule had died.

How and when she had died is not known. Perhaps – *hopefully* - she died instantly when the nose cone slammed into the desert, or perhaps she died of her injuries during the delay in reaching her. We'll never know. But there were no more attempts by the French to launch cats into space.

Two months after her flight all Félicette's tests and observations were complete.

And this is the part of this book I was dreading writing, but absolutely had to.

If this was a Disney or Netflix film, telling a fictional story, Félicette would have completed her tests and then, after a tearful farewell at the space centre - when all the people who had been involved in her mission would have gathered on the space centre steps to say goodbye and maybe hug her one last time - Félicette would have been taken home by one of the team (either a tall, skinny, awkward, geeky guy in glasses or a tall, skinny awkward, geeky girl in glasses who is revealed to be stunningly beautiful when she takes them off and lets her hair down) to begin a new and secret life with them, as a pet, not a celebrity, resuming the life she had been cheated out of when the pet shop dealer had sold her to the space agency four months earlier.

In that feelgood, heartwarming film Félicette would be shown living the life every cat deserves - leaping around a living room, chasing toys thrown for her by a laughing child; creeping through tall green grass out in the garden, stalking a doomed bird; rolling around on her owner's knee with her feet in the air, purring as her tummy is scratched and tickled, and more. It would show her growing old gracefully, in peace and safety, treasured beyond words by her owner, her celebrity status kept secret from everyone else so she could live as normal a life as possible. It would show her ageing gracefully, enjoying longer and longer naps on her owner's knee.

Eventually it would end with her padding slowly outside on a cold winter's night, to sit on the porch alone and take a last look up at the stars she had touched before going back inside and passing away peacefully in her cosy bed, looking into and warmed by the dancing flames of a flickering fire…

But Félicette wasn't a character from a film. She was real. And in real life there was no happy ending for her.

When a distraught pet owner is told by a caring vet that there is nothing more to be done, that the kindest thing they can do for their sick, beloved companion is to say goodbye. When the last scrap of hope they have been clinging on to is taken away, there are polite, vanilla terms for what comes next. The cat has to be:

Euthanised.

Put to sleep.

Let go.

But Félicette wasn't sick. She was in perfect health. In fact after all her training and dieting – apart from the long metal wires embedded in her brain of course - she'd probably never been healthier or fitter in her life. She had many good years ahead of her, and an unknown but not insignificant number of her nine lives remaining.

But she would never live them.

There's no easy way to put this. Two months after returning from her spaceflight Félicette was killed so the mission scientists could carry out a post-mortem on her to see how her body had been affected by her trip into space.

How she was killed is not recorded in any documents, reports or accounts I've come across. Most likely it was by the usual humane method, by lethal injection. I certainly hope so. It will nag at me forever not knowing for sure.

There's an image I can't get out of my head: Félicette lying on a cold metal table in a lab somewhere, being held still while someone – maybe even someone she had trusted - pushed the needle into her that would end her life. As she began to feel drowsy did they treat her kindly? Did they stroke her? Did they talk softly to her, to ease her on her way? Or did they just hold her still in silence, too ashamed to speak to her as her too short life ebbed away, or, worse, not moved at all? When she closed her bright, intelligent eyes for the last time did she see them looking back at her, their faces streaked with guilty tears, or did they all look away, too ashamed to face her and to look into the dimming eyes of the quiet, beautiful creature they had betrayed? And when she had passed away were they respectful, and let her rest in peace for a while, or did they reach for their scalpels and set to work straight away?

Either way, Félicette was killed so the mission scientists could examine her insides to see if her organs had been affected in any way by her brief exposure to space. Unsurprisingly, they hadn't. They learned, they would later admit, nothing from the autopsy and very little from the flight itself.

And *after* that? Was Félicette buried somewhere, with the respect she was due, that she had earned, or was she just disposed of, wrapped up in a bag, bundled down a refuse chute and dumped into a furnace? We'll probably never know.

I'm not sure I want to.

SIX

FÉLICETTE'S LEGACY

Almost 60 years have passed since Félicette's flight. It's now lost in the mists of space exploration history, far behind the daring, white-knuckle flights of Mercury and Gemini; behind the legendary Apollo missions that landed people on the Moon; behind the launch and fiery crash of Skylab; behind the flights of the elegant Space Shuttle fleet and the horrible deaths of the Columbia and Challenger astronauts; behind the orbital assembly of the International Space Station; behind the birth of "New Space" with its Thunderbirds-like reusable rockets that land back at their launch sites or even on barges out at sea.

After more than half a century, is it possible to look back and ask "Was it worth it"?

Yes, it is.

And no, it wasn't.

The French obviously – and, we must believe, genuinely – thought that after sending a rat into space, launching a more advanced animal like a cat into the heavens would teach them a lot more about that unforgiving, lethal environment and help them advance their medical science and engineering enough to bring forward the glorious day when a French astronaut would follow Gagarin and Shepard into space.

The positioning of the electrodes stuck on and inserted into Félicette shows they believed that they would learn about how the heart and brain were affected by being in space, and could then use that data to make travelling into space safer for human beings.

So, after Félicette's flight did the French proudly join the Space Race with a giant leap of their own? No.

Did the world watch a French astronaut climbing into a French capsule on top of a French rocket and blasting off into space? No.

After her death, were highly-detailed scientific papers written about Félicette's flight that led to advances in space medicine and spacecraft construction? No.

Ok.

Well, at the very least, having learned lessons from Félicette's flight – and autopsy – surely the French sent *more* cats into space, in more humane conditions, on flights that gathered even more data, before returning them safely to Earth, where they lived out the rest of their lives peacefully? Right?

No. As I said in the previous chapter, after the tragic failure of the second "space cat" mission, just days after Félicette's, the French stopped using cats and, following the lead of other countries, moved on to monkeys. After a lull of four years, in March 1967 two monkeys – "Martine" and "Pierette" – flew into space onboard Vesta rockets, more powerful derivatives of the Veronique rockets used to launch Félicette and her unnamed successor. After their return the project seems to have become rather muddled, with no real direction, and biological flights were stopped. They resumed in the mid-1970s, by which time France was co-operating on space research with Russia.

But no more cats ever flew into space.

What was the *point* of it all then?

Was anything learned from Félicette's flight?

What did she die for?

I haven't been able to find one quote in one book, paper or report making a positive statement about Félicette's flight. It seems her mission, and her death, didn't really contribute anything of any use or importance at all.

Years after Laika's flight, when all the propaganda had turned to whispers on the wind and the truth about her awful death in orbit had been revealed, one of the scientists involved in her mission made a painful but honest admission.

"The more time passes, the more I'm sorry about it. We shouldn't have done it. We did not learn enough from the mission to justify the death of the dog."

I wonder how many of the team behind Félicette's flight thought the same thing.

SEVEN

FÉLICETTE REMEMBERED

It's fair to say that a whole memorabilia industry has sprang up to commemorate – and cash in on - Laika's flight. "Space" Collectors – and there are many of them – are always on the lookout for new items to add to their Laika collections. There are Laika books, paintings, toys, posters, soft toys, cufflinks, ties, t-shirts, cups, goblets and mugs, plates, etc. Basically anything you can imagine being produced before or after a Royal Wedding, there is a Laika equivalent somewhere out there, adorned with an image of the first living creature to orbit the Earth.

But what about Félicette? Was she celebrated in the same way?

No.

A special postcard was produced and distributed, which is quite the collector's item today. It bears a large photo of Félicette staring off wistfully to the left, above a handwritten message: "*Thank you for your participation in my success of 18 October 1963*" It is signed with a stamped pawprint, which is cute but I'm pretty sure is not real.

Félicette's flight was also commemorated on a number of postage stamps produced by former French colonies, but not until quite some years later. The most famous of these is a stamp produced by the Comaro Islands in 1992 as part of a series of stamps commemorating "space animals" (the others in the series show Laika of course and Ham, the chimpanzee). The very colourful and attractive 150F Comaro stamp shows a Veronique rocket and the face of a black and white cat that looks a lot – but not exactly – like Félicette. Unfortunately the cat is called "Felix" on the stamp, and not Félicette.

In fact, if you look closely, **all** the stamps produced to commemorate Félicette's flight call her "Felix".

Why? Who was this mysterious "Felix"?

This is yet another odd twist in the tail of Félicette's… tale.

If you research Félicette on Google you'll find websites and blogs that tell the story of how Félicette was actually *not* the prime "Space Cat" candidate but was the back-up to another cat, a male cat called "Felix". Legend has it that the night before the Veronique rocket was due to blast-off, Felix, less than impressed by the prospect of being crammed into a tiny capsule and sent thundering up into the sky, carried out a daring feline version of the Great Escape and fled from the launch site, vanishing into the night, never to be seen again, leaving Félicette to take his place and become the first cat to go into space, with all that entailed. This has been disproved elsewhere (besides, I said earlier that all the cats obtained for training were *female* because of their more gentle nature, remember?), and it's now pretty much accepted that Felix didn't actually exist and this is just a shaggy dog – or cat – story.

But bizarrely, even though he never existed, the imaginary Felix is now part of Félicette's story, and the people who designed and produced the stamps seem to have been either misinformed by those higher up or they just didn't bother to check the details. Whatever happened, it's just one more way in which poor Félicette has been airbrushed out of the history of space exploration.

Another stamp, a 600F stamp produced by the Republic of Niger in 1999, shows a Veronique rocket with a black and white cat to its left, but it's not quite right: Félicette was a short-haired black and white Tuxedo cat, but the cat shown on the stamp is very clearly a long-haired cat. It looks more like Chewbacca than Félicette. It is a nice stamp tho.

The third stamp commemorating Félicette's flight was produced by Chad, in 1997. This stamp celebrates "Space Pioneers", and is dominated by artwork showing the crew of Apollo 11. Just beneath a grinning Neil Armstrong you can see an equally happy-looking dog that is supposed to be Laika but actually looks nothing like her, and to not-actually-Laika's right is the same artwork of Félicette used on the Comaro Islands stamp. However, yet again, the cat is labelled as "Felix".

So much for the stamps. What else can the Space Collector find if they want something in their collection that commemorates Félicette's flight?

There are lots of "unofficial" items out there, produced not by any individual or office related to the French Space Agency, past or present, but by creative people – usually cat lovers - who have been personally moved by Félicette's story and have been inspired to make something to celebrate it. Another Google search will fill your screen with images of t-shirts, rubber stamps, lithographs, badges and other things, usually available for purchase from their maker's website. There are some really lovely items available online, showing just how much Félicette's story continues to inspire and move people today, more than half a century after her historic flight, and I invite you to take a look at these yourself when you have time.

Enjoy a tipple? You can actually buy Félicette *wine*, produced in the south west of France, by the Alliance company. The bottles have very striking and unusual labels featuring a pair of cats wearing Mercury-type silver spacesuits. You can buy red, white or rose Félicette wines, which are described on the company's website as being "elegant, refreshing and delightful" and "perfect for by the glass as an aperitif or with food". I'll have to try and track some down – purely for research purposes, of course…

One item that has caught collectors' eye is a tea towel. Now, tea towels aren't very exciting, it's true, and you might think they're not a very respectful tribute to a space explorer either, but this particular tea towel is an important part of Félicette's story because it finally led to her being honoured appropriately, with a statue, 56 years after Félicette herself flew into space. We'll get to that shortly.

The tea towel is actually "wrong" in many different ways. For a start it is clearly a Russian product – featuring bold Russian artwork and text in a stereotypical Russian font – which gives the impression that the first cat in space was Russian and not French. The date shown on the towel is also wrong. It was produced in 1997 to commemorate the 50th anniversary of the flight of the "first cat in space"… which actually took place in 1963, so it was produced four years too late.

But worst of all, the cat shown on the tea towel looks absolutely – and I mean absolutely – NOTHING like Félicette.

The cat shown on the tea towel is a young tabby, little older than a kitten. Where Félicette was black and white, the cat on the towel is more of a brown or even ginger and white, and has none of Félicette's distinctive facial markings either.

But you know, for all its faults and mistakes that tea towel is a nice product, and I suppose you could say "it means well." And it did lead, as I said, to Félicette being honoured properly, with a statue. How?

FÉLICETTE'S STATUE

A couple of years ago a British designer, Matthew Serge Guy, came across the tea towel and was fascinated by it. Like many people (including myself!) he was aware that the Russians had sent dogs into space, including Laika of course, but had no idea they'd sent a cat too.

After doing a little research Matthew learned how inaccurate the tea towel was, and that the true story behind the first cat to fly into space was as fascinating as it was tragic. A cat lover himself, Matthew was surprised to learn that, unlike Laika, Ham and other animals that had flown into space, Félicette had not been honoured with a statue or even a plaque. He decided to set that wrong right, and set up a Kickstarter crowd-funding project to fund the design, construction and display of a statue of Félicette which would honour her memory, and sacrifice, far better than any tea towel or stamp could.

Matthew actually reached his financial target quite quickly, but that was the easy part. He then had to find a sculptor, work with them on designs, find a display location, and much more besides.

But eventually, on December 17ᵗʰ 2019, after almost three years of hard work, and after attracting support from all around the world, Matthew's vision became a reality when a bronze statue of Félicette was unveiled in a ceremony at the campus of the International Space University (ISU) in Strasbourg, attended by various dignitaries including astronaut Helen Sharman.

The statue – which is on display in the "Pioneers Gallery", close to a bust of Yuri Gagarin - is very striking, and features a cat sitting upright on top of a world globe, staring up into the sky. The statue is symbolic rather than realistic: the cat doesn't look anything like Félicette herself, as it is of a sleek, short-haired cat rather than a long-haired cat like Félicette, but that doesn't matter. It's a tribute to her, and her sacrifice, and that's what counts.

Strangely, Matthew wasn't there at the statue's unveiling ceremony – which I find extremely odd – and he didn't even see photos of the ceremony until I sent him some which had been sent to me by one of the people who had been there. Matthew told me, with his characteristic modesty and politeness, that it "wasn't about him" which is true enough, but seeing as the statue would never have happened *without* him I think it was grossly unfair that he wasn't invited along as a VIP guest and allowed to whip away the black cloth in person. I really hope he gets to go across to the ISU at some point and see the statue for himself.

If *I* ever make it over there I'll be sure to pat Félicette on the head on his behalf.

EIGHT

PIONEER CATS OF THE PAST

Having read Félicette's story, I expect you're now asking two questions (apart from "HOW COULD THEY DO THAT TO A CAT???"):

When will *another* cat fly into space?

And when they do, *where* will they *go*?

I've no doubt that another cat *will* travel into space one day, perhaps even in the next 50 years or so, but this time it will be under very different circumstances. They won't go as an experiment; they won't go as a payload, or package. They'll be taken there as a companion and a fellow traveller. And they won't be killed when they get back.

If they come back.

Why am I so sure? Because throughout history, wherever human beings have gone they've taken cats with them, and so when people – and by people I mean everyday people, people like you and me, not professional astronauts - eventually go up to live in space stations, then set up homes on the Moon and eventually on Mars too, they will take cats with them, for companionship, company, and because that's what settlers and explorers have *always* done.

Just like dogs, cats have always been the companions of the brave and the bold. The Vikings liked to hang out with cats, which is why cats feature in their mythology. Cats were often carried onboard Viking ships to protect their food stores from rodents as they sailed around Europe, and cats lived with Vikings in their homes too, carrying out the same very important job. (It seems not all Vikings were animal lovers though. Perhaps unsurprisingly, excavations of settlements have shown that cats were also bred and then killed for their fur, which was used in clothing to protect people against the cold). The Norse gods were cat fans too. The goddess Freya – who was kept very busy being the goddess of fertility, domesticity and womanhood, and was also strongly associated with sorcery, magic, war and death – rode in a chariot that was pulled not by horses but by a pair of huge male cats, Bygul and Trjegull, who were gifts from Thor, the God of Thunder, himself.

Centuries later, when the pioneering families of the late 1800s crossed the United States in their covered wagons, juddering and shuddering along the famous Oregon Trail and many others, they took cats with them. Not as companions or pets – there was little room for mawkish sentimentality in those cramped wagons – but so that when they eventually reached their destination and built their new homes they would have an efficient form of pest control with them.

For countless years before that, cats lived on sailing ships, fulfilling the same role. Wherever those ships went, be it the coast of the United States or the coral reef-crusted shores of Australia, cats went with them and built lives there. Some died when their ships sank in accidents or were sunk deliberately in wartime. When the Titanic set sail on her maiden voyage in 1912 a cat called Jenny was living in its galley, along with her kittens. Sadly, the whole family died when the Titanic broke apart and sank after its collision with the iceberg.

And speaking of ice, a surprising number of cats travelled to the desolate, wind-whipped ice plains of Antarctica. Most will remain anonymous forever, but the stories of a handful are well known.

MRS CHIPPY

Mrs Chippy was a tabby cat that accompanied the explorer Shackleton on his ill-fated expedition to Antarctica onboard the Endeavour in 1914. Mrs Chippy wasn't actually Shackleton's cat, and wasn't actually female either; the cat was affectionately given that nickname by members of the Endurance's crew because of the way it followed its *real* owner, ship's carpenter Harry "Chippy" McNish, around the ship like a doting wife, and the way McNish was devoted to the cat, too.

The expedition members all grew extremely fond of Mrs Chippy, and acknowledged the cat's bravery and resilience when the expedition ground to a halt and their ship became trapped in the south polar ice. But when the Endurance began to break up under the pressure of the crushing ice, forcing the expedition team to begin an epic trek across the icy wastelands on foot, Shackleton, seeking to preserve the lives of his men above everything else, ordered all items unnecessary for their survival and rescue to be left behind. Mrs Chippy, along with several pups, was ordered to be shot. McNish never forgave his Captain and Commander for that and bitterly held it against him during the rest of the journey and after, too. McNish died destitute, but today his grave in New Zealand features a lifesize statue of Mrs Chippy, reuniting them, which is only fair.

In fact, Shackleton seems to have been something of a jinx for cats. In 1921, seven years after his ill-fated 1914 expedition to the Antarctic in the "Endeavour", Shackleton journeyed there again, this time in the "Quest". It was to be his final expedition south, and his crew included a dog and a cat, called *Query* and *Questie* respectively. Photographs showing Questie being held aloft by crew members suggest she was little more than a kitten when the Quest set sail, and sadly she was destined not to grow much older. Records of the expedition tell how Questie "had a fit" and jumped overboard, with no hope of rescue. Poor Query fared no better: the dog slipped on the slick deck and was lost overboard too.

I imagine cats and dogs gave Shackleton a wide berth once he got back to England, don't you?

Going back briefly to Mrs Chippy, she wasn't the first cat to reach Antarctica. In fact, that icy continent seems to have been something of a magnet for fearless felines. The brilliant "Purr-n-Fur" UK website tells how, in 1820, almost a century before Mrs Chippy's journey there, an unnamed cat was forced to spend a harsh winter there when the sealing ship "Cora" ran aground and was wrecked on the rocky shore of the appropriately-named "Desolation Island". Thankfully, unlike poor Mrs Chippy, the cat was kept alive by its human friends until it was eventually rescued and returned to England.

"Purr-n-Fur" also tells the tales of other Antarctic cats, such as *Nansen*, a black and white kitten that sailed to the icy continent on board the vessel Belgica in 1897. When the ship became trapped in the ice – as Endeavour would be, seventeen years later - poor Nansen didn't take it well and had something of a mental breakdown, and eventually died. Then, in 1901, on the Swedish Antarctic Expedition under the command of a Captain Larsen, two cats sailing on the ship Antarctica had to be rescued by the crew when it too became trapped in the ice and sank. One died while the crew was waiting for rescue, but the other survived, living in a makeshift hut on the ice and eating penguin and fish, and made it home to Sweden and a hero's welcome.

The great polar explorer Scott also seems to have had something of a "thing" for taking cats with him. "Purr-n-Furr" again describes how the adventurer took cats with him on an expedition in 1901 and on his doomed expedition of 1910, which saw a black cat called *Nigger* accompanying him and his team onto the ice. By all accounts Nigger was a much-loved companion for the explorers, and when he died in 1912 – washed overboard during a storm – they were very upset by the loss of their friend.

What about today? A hundred years after Mrs Chippy sailed there onboard the Endeavour, are the snowy plains of Antarctica criss-crossed by tracks of tiny pawprints? Well no, not any more. As recently as the late 1970s cats could be found living in research bases in Antarctica, but none have been allowed there for many years now to protect the local wildlife from their "attention". Again, the excellent "Purr-n-Furr" website has been a goldmine of information about "Antarctican Cats", and if you're interested in learning about them you should definitely pay it a visit.

Without it I would never have learned about *Judith*, a tabby cat who may or may not have been the great *great* grand-daughter of Mrs Chippy, the cat that went on Shackleton's expedition to the South Pole. Nor would I have read the fascinating stories of Antarctican cats *Tubby, Tiddles* or *Ginge*.

The site has tales of many others too, and as a source of information about cats I can't recommend it highly enough.

So, there are no cats living in Antarctica now – at least *on* the continent; I'm sure a few visit onboard ships without ever setting paw on the ice. I can't help wondering if any cats have ever made it to somewhere equally inhospitable, Everest Base Camp, but my research has drawn a blank on that – so far.

CATS AT WAR

Cats have travelled to the ends of the Earth, but they have also gone to war. There are many accounts and reports of mud-caked cats keeping equally filthy First and Second World War soldiers – on both sides - company in the trenches and on the battlefields. There's even a weirdly popular Pinterest site for pictures of "Nazis with Cats".

Cats don't seem to have been too fond of going into the air during wartime tho, or associating with those who did. There are many memorable and touching photos showing young fighter pilots resting between sorties, sitting in the shadows of their Spitfires' wings, happily stroking dogs, but I've found only one photo of an RAF cat, standing on the back of a fighter, looking quite bored as it peers over the shoulder of its grinning pilot.

But, ironically for a creature that has a famous aversion to water, it seems that cats went to sea in wartime without any hesitation. It doesn't take more than a minute's searching on Google to retrieve a wealth of information about numerous cats that served on naval warships, and were adored by their crews, not just because they were useful - keeping down the numbers of rodents onboard who could gnaw through ropes and wires and contaminate or eat food supplies, and carry disease too – but because they provided them with a priceless connection to home and "normal life".

Although no cats have been allowed on Royal Navy ships since 1975, before then they were regular fixtures on sailing ships of war, and some of them have become almost legendary figures. Like Blackie, the ship's cat of the HMS Prince of Wales, who famously met and charmed Winston Churchill in 1941, and Convoy, the cat who served onboard HMS Hermione and even had its own hammock!

Of course, many cats have sailed on many ships that weren't being fired upon by other ships, submarines or planes. Between 1934 and 1937 a cat called *Lummo* travelled the 2000 miles plus from the Falkland Islands to the UK onboard the ship Penola. But that long trip was nothing compared to the travels of *Doodles*, a cat which made itself very much at home onboard the White Star liner "Cedric". During their time on the Cedric Doodles travelled more than a million miles, criss-crossing the ocean.

But even Doodles' accumulated journeys pale into insignificance when compared to the globe-trotting exploits of the grandly-named *Princess Truman Tao-Tia*. From 1959 this Siamese cat clocked up an incredible 1.5 million miles (2.4m km) onboard a ship which carried iron-ore around the world.

Today no doubt there are many cats padding across the decks of private ships, sashaying along the lush carpeted corridors of huge white ocean liners and scampering up and down the ladders and gangways of the massive cargo ships that transport goods across the world, and who knows how many cats accompany their celebrity owners when they set out to sea in their luxury yachts and sailing boats.

But what of the future? Will cats ever leave the Earth altogether, as Félicette did?

CATS IN THE AIR

It might take a while, but I have absolutely no doubt that they will. After all, while most cats through the ages have been quite content to keep all four paws on the ground, since the dawn of the "Age of Flight" many others have defied gravity and soared amongst the clouds.

Although they had a pet cat called *Old Mom* as children, as far as we know no cats ever flew on any of the Wright Brothers' wood and canvas planes across the sands at Kitty Hawk. However, in the years that followed many cats did take to the sky. Charles Lindbergh, famous for being the first aviator to cross the Atlantic in a plane, frequently took his cat *Patsy* with him when he flew, although she didn't accompany him on his history-making flight Anyone who has seen the classic World War II film "The Dambusters" knows that Royal Air Force pilot Wing Commander Guy Gibson was devoted to his dog *Nigger*, whose untimely end was shown so heartbreakingly in the film, but less well known us how he also frequently flew with a cat in his cockpit. Depending on which book or website you read it was called either *Windy* or (more likely, when you think about it) *Wings*.

Probably the most accomplished feline air traveller is *Hamlet*, who collected a ridiculous amount of air miles by accident. After escaping from their travel container on a flight between Toronto and London, Hamlet hid away inside the plane, and despite a comprehensive search being carried out couldn't be found. They probably assumed Hamlet had got out of the cargo altogether because the plane was kept in service, and continued to cross the skies. To everyone's amazement, seven weeks – and more than 600,000 miles (960,000km) – later Hamlet was found, trapped behind a panel in the cargo hold. Unsurprisingly, without anything to eat Hamlet had grown painfully thin, but had managed to survive by licking condensation off the panelling. Thankfully Hamlet recovered and lived out the rest of his remaining lives in comfort – and on the ground – in Norfolk.

So surely, having conquered the sky, going into space to conquer the final frontier will be just be the next logical step for cats?

Yes. But it won't happen any time soon.

NINE

FUTURE SPACE CATS

As I write this in mid-April 2022 the only spacecraft carrying crew up to and back down from space are the Russian Soyuz capsules, which are so small and cramped there genuinely is not enough room inside them to sit a cat let alone swing one. Crewed Dragon capsules, built by Elon Musk's ambitious SpaceX company, have flown several missions into space. China is developing a Dragon-like capsule capable of carrying people too.

But at the moment – and for the foreseeable future - there are only two places for such capsules to go to – a pair of space stations in orbit around the Earth. One belongs to China, the other is an international project. The International Space Station, or the "ISS" as it's called for short, is a scientific outpost (with occasional private visitors, or "space tourists") which is hugely expensive to maintain and keep supplied.

There's absolutely no chance of us seeing any cats floating through the modules of either space station. Not real ones anyway.

But might that change in the future? Possibly. Private citizens are already sable to take trips into space – short ones, just long enough to break through that Von Karman Line and enjoy fantastic views of the Earth before coming down again – onboard small privately-built reusable capsules such as Blue

Origin's "New Shepherd" (which carried Star Trek's Captain Kirk, actor William Shatner, into space on a flight in 2021) or in "space-planes" like Virgin Galactic's. Although seats on these sightseeing flights cost a fortune, and not a small one either, there is a demand. Virgin Galactic already has a long waiting list for its flights.

Money talks, the saying goes, and money talks very loudly in the space business, so if one of the mega-wealthy passengers decides they want to take their beloved cat with them, and is willing to pay an extra few hundred thousand dollars for the privilege, I'm sure they'll be accommodated, if only for the publicity value of such a spectacle. Perhaps the *second* cat in space will be the pampered pussy of a film star or a pop singer, a well-fed Persian with its mane of fur fluffed out like an 80s rock star's perm, or a sleek Siamese with barely-open eyes..?

And after that?

At some point in the not-too-distant future space tourists will want more than just a short up-and-under to the edge of space and back again. They'll want to go into orbit, and then stay for an extended period "up there", long enough to take in the view properly and really feel like they've been into space. This will inevitably lead to the construction of "space hotels" for the wealthy to fly to and live on for at least a few days. At first these will be like small submarines, little more than a pair of pressurised tin can modules joined together, with an airlock, a modest "guest room" and a viewing gallery, but over time these will give way to larger constructions with multiple rooms and the capacity to house multiple guests for weeks at a time. Then I am sure we will see cats going up into space, accompanying their super-rich owners on their trips of a lifetime, if only to take and Share photos of them on social media, showing them silhouetted against the Earth, staring out wistfully at the stars or miserably coughing up hairballs as they somersault in zero gravity…

But one day it won't just be the super-rich who take trips into space. Eventually travelling into space will become much cheaper and much safer, and as demand for trips into and stays in space increases the types of people who will leave Earth will change too. As space finally "opens up" just as they had to with share airplanes and cruise ships in the past the millionaires and billionaires will have to share Earth orbit with everyone.

And then there are the "creative types".

Not all the pioneers who travelled across the United States to explore and settle the "Wild West" were rugged adventurers looking for adventure and a new life. Some were writers and artists who were drawn to the west by its wide open spaces, huge skies and stunningly beautiful landscapes, and a desire to capture them in words and in paint. The same will be true of space.

Many of the most successful and famous writers in history were cat owners, so it's not outrageous to think that some of the writers who travel into space in the not-too-distant future will be too. After all, Ernest Hemingway's cats *Crazy Christian* and *Friendless Brother* kept him company while he wrote. Long before then, legendary author Mark Twain had several cats, including *Buffalo Bill* and *Sour Mash*. The infamous romantic poet Lord Byron was accompanied on his travels around Europe by a cat called *Beppo*, Edgar Allan Poe's cat *Catarina* inspired his classic story "Black Cat" and Charles Dickens looked up from his writing to see *The Master's Cat* watching over him. Writer TS Elliot's famous book 'Old Possum's Book of Practical Cats', the inspiration behind the musical "Cats", was itself inspired by his own cat *Jellylorum*. Scottish writer Sir Walter Scott, author of The Waverly Novels and poems such as "The Lord of The Isles" had a cat called *Hinse* which enjoyed tormenting and fighting with his hounds, but one day Hinse picked on the wrong dog and was attacked and killed by it. And Victor Hugo, famous for the classic French revolutionary tale "Les Miserables", was owned by a cat called *Mouche*.

While the writers are tapping away on their keyboards or tablets, struggling to find the right words to describe how majestic the view of Earth is from several hundred kilometres above the ground orbit, or waxing lyrical about how much brighter and more plentiful the stars are from high above the pollution-choked atmosphere, artists will be using their creative skills to capture and communicate to others the beauty of space, and I'm sure some will have cats by their sides. After all, throughout history cats have provided artists with companionship and inspiration - although sadly my favourite artist, Albert Bierstadt, who painted the sweeping landscapes, meandering canyons and towering mountain ranges of the

American West in the 19th century didn't take a cat with him on his expeditions across the vast Sierra Nevada, around the snow-capped Rocky Mountains and through stunning-ly-beautiful Yosemite Valley.

As with writers, it would be impossible to list all of them here, but many artists had cats beside them while they worked at their easels, including Gustav Klimt (*Katze*) and Picasso (*Minou*). Matisse had no less than three cats, *Minouche*, *Loussi* and *Le Puce*. Thankfully Salvador Dali didn't show a melted version of his exotic ocelot cat Babou in any of his paintings, but Andy Warhol did feature his cat, *Sam*, on several of his artworks,

Another group of people will fly into space one day – but only once it's proven to be totally safe (or as safe as possible) to do: politicians. All through history politicians have trav-elled to exotic, even dangerous places, but only after other braver and less risk-averse individuals have been to those places first and shown them to be safe, or made them safe for others, and I'm sure space will be no different. So once there are hotels and space stations orbiting high above the Earth safe enough for 'normal' people to visit and spend time on, politicians will follow, eager to be photographed shaking hands with the hotel managers and owners and their guests.

Will any of them take cats with them to the final frontier? Well, if history is anything to go by then yes, I think they will. Many famous politicians of the past owned – and, to be fair, loved – cats, and I don't think it's too huge a stretch of the imagination to picture politicians visiting the space stations and hotels of the future posing with their cats on their laps as they swap grinning smiles with the multi-billionaire devel-opers who funded and built them.

Here in the UK cats have been prominent political figures since the 1500s, or at least have supported them. Any famous British Prime Minister you can name almost certainly had a cat wandering around No 10 Downing Street during their stay there. Neville Chamberlain and Clement Attlee both had cats, and through the darkest hours of World War II the great Winston Churchill was no doubt calmed and comforted by the presence of his appropriately-named cat *Nelson*. Between 1989 and 1997 a cat called Humphrey – named after a Machiavellian character from a much-loved satitrical political TV comedy called "Yes Minister", watched by millions at the time – prowled the corridors of No 10 and watched Prime Ministers Margaret Thatcher, John Major and Tony Blair come and go.

The current feline occupant of 10 Downing Street is *Larry*, who took up the new official position of "Chief Mousser to the Cabinet Office" in 2011. Since taking up his brief he has served under Prime Ministers David Cameron, Theresa May and Boris Johnson. More likely they feel they have served under *him*; you know what cats are like…

Across the vast Atlantic, many US Presidents have had cats. Abraham Lincoln was devoted to his cat *Tabby*, and Theodore Roosevelt owned two cats, *Tom Quartz* and *Slippers*. Ronald Reagan – often pictured in a very macho pose, perhaps in a cowboy hat or astride a horse – shared his eventful terms in the White House with two cats called *Cleo* and *Sara*. Years later a grinning President Bill Clinton brought another cat to the White House. *Socks,* an adopted tray black and white tuxedo cat, soon became a media and public favourite, visiting schools and hospitals and receiving fan mail from around the world. Socks was featured on international stamps and in many books, had songs written about him, appeared in

cartoons and even had a title: "*First Cat of the United States!*"
By the time the Clintons left the White House in 2009 it's
fair to say that Socks had became the first feline star of the
internet age, but he didn't accompany the Clintons when
they moved house, due to, shall we say, "creative differences"
with their dog. Bill Clinton's replacement, George W Bush,
brought his cat *India* into the White House, but neither Presidents Obama or Trump shared their occupancy of the Oval
Office with a cat. I don't think anyone was surprised that
Trump didn't have a cat, or a dog, with them in the White
House. Famously Trump had never owned a pet in his life,
which says a lot about him I think.

Today another cat stalks the corridors of the White House
- President Biden's adopted grey and white tabby farm cat,
Willow. The Bidens originally had a dog, big boisterous *Major*
but what have been tactfully described as "biting issues"
meant Major was sent to live with another family elsewhere,
much to Willow's relief, no doubt…

TEN

INTERPLANETARY CATS

One day, who knows how far in the future, people will travel to worlds beyond Earth, and cats will surely accompany them, just as they did to America, Australia and Antarctica. Try and stop them.

It might take several generations for it to happen. At the moment it seems likely there will be no NASA or any other astronauts bouncing across the Moon for at least another fifteen years, and no matter what super-rich Tony Stark wannabes say, I honestly don't think we will see any boots scuffing up the red dust of Mars until 2035 at the earliest. That means no "settlers" on the Moon for another, what, half century? And no martian homesteads until 2050 or so.

But one day there will be.

One day there will be so many people working on the Moon, for such extended periods, that they will need – no, *demand* - a more domestic and "natural" environment than a sterile, cold Moon base.

The scientists, engineers and technicians working inside them and maintaining them will have to spend longer and longer away from home, and will want their families with them. As the base expands, eventually there will need to be service industries on the Moon, and inevitably leisure and entertainment facilities too. The people who work in those sectors won't be able to afford to skip back and forth between the Earth and Moon so they'll set up permanent homes there, in groups, co-operatives, and once they do they will want pets, it's inevitable. And at some point some black market entrepreneur will realise there could be a lot of money to be made from selling cats, and dogs, to people missing some of the comforts of Earth. All it will take will be to smuggle a pair of them up to the Moon, let Nature take its course, and count the cash as it flows in as their underground black market pet empire grows…

And then, one day, **Mars**.

Mars is a long, long way away, a flight of 6 months' duration as opposed to the 3 day hop to the Moon, so for a long time the only people going there will be professional astronauts and scientists, dispatched to study the planet and look for life there. Just as there is in Antarctica today there will be very strict rules about contaminating Mars with primitive Earth lifeforms, so there's no way a cat will be allowed to go there! But eventually, who knows when in the future, a decision will be made that it's time to stop studying Mars like a fossil and quarantining it and start *settling* it, spreading out across it just as the American pioneers did, and then large ships crammed full of engineers, technicians and construction workers, ordinary people, will set off for it, ready to begin the construction of the first martian town. That will take a long time, a *very* long time. I'm sure no-one alive today will see it. But one day there will be families living on Mars, raising kids there, carving out lives there. And like those pioneering families of the Wild West they will have food stores to protect and vermin to catch. And their kids will want pets. So, eventually, there will be cats on Mars.

Perhaps, on October 18th 2113, on the 150th anniversary of Félicette's journey into space, a cat will sit quietly by a window in a module standing out on the rocky surface of Mars, watching the sunset, and as the twilight turns the martian sky a lovely shade of blue they will see a beautiful "Evening Star" shining above the faraway hills and volcano peaks, lantern-bright: Earth, the home of Félicette, the first cat to fly into space.

ELEVEN

SCI-FI SPACE CATS

When a cat does eventually make it off Earth, to an orbiting space hotel, the Moon or Mars, they'll be following in the pawprints of some very illustrious predecessors. Although Félicette is the only cat to have flown into space in real life, other cats have swiped a claw at the final frontier – in science fiction.

Science fiction literature is full of space-faring cats. In David Webber's popular books his space navy heroine Honor Harrington has *Nimitz*, a telepathic cat, for a best friend. Anne McCaffrey, best known for her Pern books featuring brave dragon-riders on a faraway alien world, wrote memorable stories about Barque cats, cats bred specifically to live on spacecraft. In his Known Space series, Larry Niven's fearsome *Kzinti* are a bloodthirsty race of giant, intelligent cats, a bit like a cross between Klingons and warrior space tigers.

But the best known sci-fi cats are the feisty felines who have appeared on TV and in films. Of all the various universes out there, the Star Trek universe has had the most cats. In one episode of the original series, Captain Kirk, Dr McCoy and all the rest of the USS Enterprise's crew were surprised when the emotion-suppressing Vulcan Mr Spock – yes, the one with the pointy ears – bonded with a black cat, that turned out to be a shape-shifting alien. In another episode from the original series Gary 7, a mysterious James Bond-like character from the far future, had a partner - a slinky black cat called *Isis*, and the two of them ran rings around the Enterprise crew as he tried to avert World War 3. If you know anything about Star Trek you won't be amazed to hear that Isis also turned out to be a shape-changing alien, transforming from a black cat into a very curvy, scantily-clad young woman...

Later series set in the Star Trek universe also featured cats. In Star Trek: The Next Generation Commander Data, an android with even fewer emotions than Mr Spock, is totally devoted to his pet cat called *Spot*, to the point where he paints it and writes (*very* bad), poetry about it. A cat called *Chester* also appeared in a few episodes of the spin-off series Star Trek: Deep Space Nine.

As far as *modern* sci-fi TV is concerned one cat rules the screen. In the BBC comedy series of the same name, all but one of the crew of the mining ship "Red Dwarf" are killed in an accident and when the lone survivor, Lister, emerges from hibernation he finds that millions of years have passed. In that time the offspring of his cat, Frankenstein, have evolved beyond all recognition; he comes face to face with *Cat*, a sassy, jive-talking, dandily-dressed humanoid cat that dances and jazz hands his way through the ship like James Brown. He's a brilliant comic creation, and at the time of writing is still in the show.

On the big screen cats haven't ventured into space that often. In the 1978 Disney film "The Cat From Outer Space" a UFO crashes in the United States and after it is taken into custody by the military the spaceship's pilot, an alien cat called *Jake*, enlists the help of a scientist and her cat to retrieve it.

But the most famous – and luckiest – cat to have gone into space in a science fiction film has to be *Jones*, a ginger and white cat in the 1979 film "Alien". After investigating a distress signal transmitted from an alien planet, the crew of the mining ship (what is it with cats and space mining ships?) Nostromo are picked off one by one by a terrifying and merciless alien stowaway, a couple of them actually while they are looking for Jones, it has to be said. Eventually only one crew member, Ripley, is left alive, and after she manages to kill the alien she and Jones go into hibernation for the long trip back to Earth. In the sequel, "Aliens", Ripley reluctantly heads back to the alien planet to fight more of the aliens, but Jonesy, very wisely, stays safely on Earth.

TWELVE

CAT CONSTELLATIONS

Cats go missing all the time. Walk down any street and you'll probably come across a poster stuck to a lamp-post or pinned to a tree asking people to check their sheds and gardens for a beloved pet that has wandered off. But did you know that many, many years ago a cat went missing from the night sky – and it never came back..?

Today there is a lot of concern about the way our night sky is under threat from "constellations" of artificial satellites thrown up into space by multi-billionaires and mega-companies. Many astronomers, both amateur and professional, are becoming very worried that the very appearance of the night sky itself will change as hundreds, then thousands and perhaps eventually even tens of thousands of small satellites are put into orbit to buzz around Earth like metallic bees. Not only will they be visible to the naked eye, but they will carve trails across long exposure images of the sky taken by professional telescopes studying the universe. "These selfish people need to stop using the night sky as their own personal canvas," is the cry, "no-one has the right to change the constellations we see!"

But this has happened before, and last time it was the astronomers themselves who changed the constellations, without asking for permission or approval from anyone else. Kind of.

For many centuries the names and the numbers of constellations weren't fixed. Constellations came and went as astronomers drew up their own atlases and charts, personalising the sky just as we personalise our Twitter and Facebook pages today. That all changed in 1922 when the International Astronomical Union, the IAU (cue loud booing from Pluto fans still bitter at the IAU for demoting that world to the status of "dwarf planet") decided that enough was enough and standardised the night sky, drawing up a definitive and permanent list of constellations that would never change. Today we all know the night sky as a huge jigsaw puzzle with 88 pieces, each piece a constellation, and those constellation names and identities are honoured around the world. If you break the list down, 28 constellations represent inanimate objects, 2 represent natural features and 14 represent human beings. That's about half. The other half? You probably won't be surprised to hear that they're represented by animals.

Most of those animal-related constellations are based on real life creatures. If you know where to look on Spring nights you can see mighty Leo, the Lion, prowling across the sky. On warm Summer nights it doesn't really get dark enough to see all but the brightest stars, but you can still see Cygnus the Swan and Aquila the Eagle flying together in Red Arrows-style close formation down the Milky Way's frothy star clouds around midnight. Autumn is the time to look for the twin fish of Pisces, Aries the Ram and Equuleus the Horse in the darkening sky, and by the time Winter's frosty nights roll around you can stare up and see Orion being attacked by Taurus the Bull. Elsewhere on chilly winter nights you can find a crab (Cancer) scuttling across the heavens, a giraffe (Camelopardalis) striding elegantly across the heavens and, of course, not one but two bears – Ursa Major and Ursa Minor – swaying along on their way as they lumber around the Pole Star.

The remaining half dozen or so animal constellations represent magical or mysterious creatures from myth and legend. Again, if you know where and when to look you, at various times during the year you can find a fearsome Dragon, a graceful Unicorn, a fire-bathed Phoenix and many other fantastic creatures "up there".

But there is a glaring omission from the list of animal-related constellations. Even though they hold such an important place in the hearts of countless millions of people – and have spread to every corner of the Internet and the real world too, as we saw in the previous chapter - there is no domestic cat in the night sky. It's an outrage!

Perhaps. But there *used* to be a cat in the night sky, and to learn about its tail – sorry, tale – we have to go back in time, long before Félicette's flight, almost two centuries into the distant past...

1799 was a landmark year, an epic year some would say, and if time travel is ever invented then there will be a queue of TARDIS's waiting to go back to it. Some time travellers will be drawn to America, to witness the first President of the United States, George Washington, taking his last breath shortly before Christmas. Braver time tourists will head for Europe, where the bloody Napoleonic Wars were reaching a climax bringing to an end the French Revolution. But no-one, I'm sure, would be desperate to buy a ticket to pop into existence in the peaceful but cluttered study of French astronomer Joseph Jerome de Lalande, as he picked up his quill to write to his fellow astronomer Johann Bode with a rather outrageous suggestion - unless they were cat loving astronomers, that is.

Lalande, an accomplished astronomer who is best known now for having *almost* discovered Neptune, was a cat lover, and as such was very frustrated that while there were no fewer than three dogs in the night sky there was no domestic cat. Knowing that Bode was drafting a new star atlas, because he had helped with observations being used to compile it, Lalande suggested that Bode should include a new constellation representing a cat. Bode agreed, and when his beautifully detailed "Uranographia" atlas appeared two years later there was a cat, Felis, stretched out next to the curled body of Hydra. To be honest, Felis looks more like a guinea pig than a cat, but it's the thought that counts. Lalande must have been delighted, and perhaps before he died, just four years later, it was some comfort to him that he had redressed a terrible celestial injustice by placing one of his beloved feline friends in the heavens for all to see, or at least for those who flipped through the pages of Bode's star atlas to see.

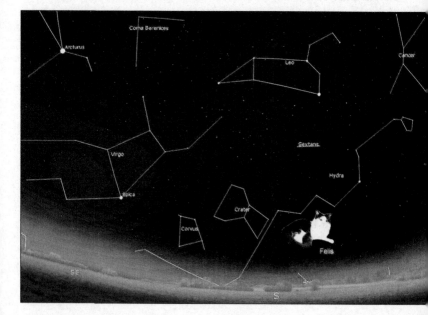

Felis actually remained an accepted constellation for the next 123 years, appearing in various star atlases, including, most famously, Jamieson's stunningly beautiful "Celestial Atlas" of 1822, and on that chart Felis actually *looked* like a cat. However, like many adventurous cats do, Felis was living on borrowed time...

In 1922, forty years or so before Félicette's flight, the IAU decided that the night sky had just gotten too messy and too confusing. (In 2006 the IAU would unilaterally decide that the solar system itself had gotten too messy and too confusing too, and would demote Pluto to a dwarf planet). The IAU was determined to "tidy up" the sky, to make sense out of the chaos and bring everything, and everyone, into line, and agreed to formalise the number, names and identities of the constellations so everyone, everywhere would use the same ones – the ones *they* approved of. That meant some of the small, quirky and eccentric constellations would have to go. When advising astronomer Flammarion suggested grumpily that Felis was too small and too vague to remain a constellation it was duly removed in the IAU's constellation cull, its faint stars absorbed into nearby Hydra, and that was that. Felis was no more.

And no matter how many Missing posters cat-loving astronomers pin to crazily-spinning pulsars or staple to sparkling star clusters, Felis will never come back.

Although it's no consolation to cat lovers, astronomers or otherwise, Felis wasn't the only animal constellation to be removed from the sky. There used to be an owl ("Noctua"), a reindeer ("Rangifr") and even a toad ("Bufo") in the sky. And what a shame that we can no longer look up on a clear night and see Limox, the Slug, shining down on us...

There is some good news: a trace of the original constellation of Felis remains. In 2018 the IAU – perhaps feeling guilty about what it had done almost a century earlier, but probably not – announced that the 4th magnitude star HD85951 in the constellation of Hydra would be officially known as "Felis".

HD85951 is an orange giant star with a diameter more than 80 times that of our own Sun, so maybe it's not too overly poetic to think of it as a big, fluffy orange tabby cat sleeping in front of a fire, 614 light years away from us, out in the cold depths of space.

So, sadly there is no domestic cat in our night sky today. We can't go out on a clear night, look up and see a cat shape in the sky to remind us of Félicette.

But that might change in the future…

THIRTEEN

FÉLICETTE HONOURED
IN AN ALIEN SKY..?

With NASA planning to send astronauts back to the Moon in a few years (hmm, we'll see #1...) with its Artemis program, and Elon Musk predicting SpaceX astronauts will race across Mars in electric Tesla rovers within his lifetime (hmmm, we'll see #2!), it seems people will be looking up at the constellations from other worlds before too long. But both those destinations are so close to the Earth that will be no change in the appearance of the constellations. When the first Artemis mission eventually lands on the Moon, and the first female astronaut to walk on its surface looks up she'll see a familiar sky, with all of the same constellations such as Leo and Ursa Major that she grew up beneath on Earth. Likewise, when the first astronauts to land on Mars look up at the sky after their first sunset they will see, beyond Mars' twin moons, exactly the same constellations they saw from Earth because although Mars is much further away than the Moon it is still nowhere near far enough away to affect the appearance of the night sky.

To see entirely new constellations, people will have to travel a lot further out into space – in fact, to worlds orbiting *other stars*, many *light years* away.

Luckily, it turns out we're not short of those.

We used to know of only one family of planets orbiting a star – our own, *The* Solar System. But for centuries intellectuals had pondered the existence of others. In the 16th century the Italian philosopher Giordano Bruno wrote: "*This space we declare to be infinite… in it are an infinity of worlds of the same kind As our own.*" Two centuries later, Sir Isaac Newton confidently predicted other stars would have their own solar systems, like ours. As astronomy progressed, and telescopes and observing equipment became more powerful and more sophisticated and by the 1950s astronomers - based on their observations of stars forming, and their calculations - were convinced that other stars had their own systems of planets, moons, asteroids and comets, but they had no proof.

That, and our view of the universe and our own place in it, changed forever in 1992 when the first "exoplanets" – planets found orbiting another star – were found. Radio astronomers Aleksander Wolszczan and Dale Frail found two planets in orbit around "PSR 1257+12", a bizarre type of star called a *pulsar*. Three years later a giant planet was found in a four-day orbit around a more "normal" star, 51 Pegasi, and then the floodgates opened.

Today more than FIVE THOUSAND exoplanets have been discovered, and there are many more "candidates" waiting to be confirmed by follow-up observations. Of course, all these worlds are so stupidly, ridiculously far away that there's no chance of us ever reaching them, at least not with our current technology. But in the future, who knows? Perhaps a 22nd century Einstein or Hawking will come up with a way to accelerate spaceships to a speed that will make flights to the stars possible?

More likely, it will take centuries to discover a way to make interstellar journeys practical, and to build ships that will carry people to the stars. But I have no doubt that they will one day, and when they do make those epic journeys, just as the explorers and settlers of the past did, those star-bound explorers will take animals with them, including, inevitably, cats.

And as those curious cats pad down the landing ramps of their ships to stand on the surfaces of those alien worlds they'll be following in the pawprints of the first cat to go into space, crammed inside a tiny rocket, launched from the middle of a desert in Africa, hundreds of years before their new home world was even discovered.

Life will be hard on those new worlds. It will take the colonists decades if not centuries to make them into homes. But I like to think that one day, many centuries from now, when the tough colonists of Dimidium (51 Pegasi b) or Aegir (Epsilon Eridani b) have finished the work needed just to keep themselves and their families alive, they will finally have time to draw up an atlas of their night sky, joining the dots of the alien stars twinkling above their strange and beautiful new home to make their *own* constellations, honouring their *own* heroes and heroines, celebrating stories, people and places with special meaning to them, they will find a small corner of the sky in which to honour the memory of a certain feline.

And every night after, as darkness falls on their settlement, plunging it into darkness, they'll look up and see a constellation shaped like a cat prowling their night sky.

The constellation of "Félicette".

FOURTEEN

FÉLICETTE POEMS

As well as writing children's books about astronomy and space I also write "astro-poetry", poetry inspired by the universe we live in and how we see and explore it. You won't be amazed to hear that Félicette's story inspired me to write some poetry about here, and here it is:

FÉLICETTE

As the YouTube vid begins she looks like any other cat:
Huge, blinking eyes; a natty tuxedo of black and white fur;
Twitching whiskers and cute button nose.
The nice man in the white coat keeps stroking her,
Petting her, tickling her behind her pointy ears like a kindly vet -
And then you see it: an obscene SCART socket embedded in her head
Where some French Frankenstein screwed a metal plate
Into her fragile skull and wriggled wires into her brain,
Hoping to learn how being in space would affect her thoughts and feelings.
How the hell did they *think* she'd feel,
Crammed into a tiny metal crate and hurled up into space?

After being plucked from the Paris streets she had *some*
"training".
They carried her to a centrifuge where, sealed into a space
age
Iron maiden, in a chamber with more than enough room
to swing a cat,
They twirled her round and round and round,
The sound of her crying drowned out
By the whumpf, *whumpf,* **whumpf** of the whirling
machine…

When it finally came her trip into space was brief,
Only a quick, fifteen minute/156 klick
Alan Shepard up-and-down-again,
But still far enough to make history;
Still high enough for her furry face to be
Immortalised on tea towels, mugs and stamps.
Back on Terra Firma a heroine's welcome waited,
Then three months of well-earned cuddles, hugs and
smiles

Before they cut her up like ham, slicing her clever brain
like bacon.
All in the name of "science", insisting it would help them
Launch astronauts of their own safely in years to come…
But they never did.
I know, I know… "It was a different time", you say,
"They'd never do anything like that now."
And that's true. But when I look into Felicitte's eyes,
See her blinking in black and white
I feel ashamed at the price *she* paid
For *their* curiosity.

© Stuart Atkinson 2017

I LIKE TO THINK

I like to think that, in a different corner of the Multi-
verse, you survived.
There, you didn't lift your curious eyes;
There, when He came looking for cats to send into space
He never saw your face because
In that universe you wisely stayed in the shadows
At the back of the cage, hiding out of sight
As the others leapt into the spotlight,
Meowing, dancing, prancing with delight,
No idea what he had planned as they nuzzled his hand,
Just excited to be going to a new forever home.
Silently, you watched them go, leaving you alone,
Rejected for being too dull, too sullen, too quiet
And shy, judged to be undeserving of the honour of
flying
Through the sky to play amongst the stars…

Instead *another* cat took your place in history,
Had silvery electrodes embedded in *its* brain,
Was twirled and whirled in a centrifuge, bruised like old
fruit.
They were crammed into that Iron Maiden capsule, not
you;
Shrink-wrapped in a strait-jacket of buckles, belts and
straps
Before being blasted into space,
Returning to Earth mere minutes after climbing a single
rollercoaster hump -
Then carved up like rump steak in the name of "Science".

But what happened to *you*?
I like to think that shop door opened again the next day

And this time *you* were taken away to a home of your own,
With a roaring fire to lay beside and enough head scratches
And belly rubs to last the rest of your final ninth life.

I like to think you passed away on your sad owner's lap
Peacefully, with words of love whispered in your ears,
Not drugged on a cold, stainless steel slab
And cut into pieces by "boffins" in masks.
I like to think you died of old age,
Not "euthanised" like our universe's Felicitte – betrayed and slain
By those she had trusted to keep her safe;
The same smiling women and men who softly stroked her head
For the cameras before shaving it and ramming
A shiny circuit board through her eggshell skull.
I like to think you dashed crazily about the house chasing toys,
Skidding on the floor, crashing noisily into cupboards and doors,
Nipping unprotected ankles and wrestling balls of wool
Before nestling in a young girl's arms and purring loud enough
In your sleep to drown out the sound of the TV
Showing Armstrong walking on the Moon.

© Stuart Atkinson 2019

TWO GHOSTS

When the first explorers land on Mars
They'll be met by two ghosts – the spirits of Laika and Félicette,
The first dog and cat in space.

The puzzled looks on their faces will be priceless
As they step off the ladder onto the ground and turn around
To see dusty-pawed pioneers already sitting there,
Staring back coldly and as the astronauts boldly go
Where no man - or woman - has ever gone before
They'll feel four accusing eyes boring into them.

Ignoring them as they proudly raise their flag won't work;
They'll still be there, staring, staring;
Laika with her teeth bared, Félicette's white whiskers a'twitching
Angrily, growling "Don't forget you're only here because of us.
We died so you could take your One Small Steps…"

The astronauts will pretend they're all alone as they
bounce Merrily across Ares' moaning cinnamon sands,
picking up Pitted red rocks and stones in their fat, gloved
hands, Celebrities smiling for a billion fans watching
back home on TV
While avoiding the eyes of their accusers,
One who died high above the Earth, terrified, gulping
down furnace-hot air,
The other 'euthanised' in her sleep then sliced-up
Like bacon by boffins impatient to see
How 15 minutes in space had affected the elec-
trode-studded brain
Of a tiny cat.

© Stuart Atkinson 2020

AFTERWORD

So there you have it, the story of Félicette, the first and so far only cat to go into space.

This wasn't an easy book to write and it won't have been easy for many of you to read, especially those of you with pets – not just cats – of your own. I'm sure that, like me, at some places in the story you felt so sad, upset or angry that you had to leave it and give your own pet a hug, letting them know you love them, feeling sadness and maybe even shame for what was done to Félicette in the name of science.

It's some consolation that this would not happen now. We don't need to cram monkeys, dogs or cats into little metal coffins and then push those into tiny capsules at the pointy ends of rockets to "learn about space" anymore. Human beings have been going into space for over half a century now so we know what it's like – it's a cold, dark, dangerous wasteland, an endless void that will kill the foolish, the arrogant and the unprepared any and every chance it gets. But we learned that through the experiences of humans, not from the experiences of animals, and certainly not from the experiences of a little black and white cat that had electrodes drilled into her brain and was given electric shocks during a flight in space that was not much longer than the time it takes to open a fridge door, take out a tin of cat food and spoon it into a bowl.

I said at the start of this book that it wasn't going to be your average or "normal" book about space, and now you've reached the end of it I'm sure you can see what I meant. I wrote this book as an animal-lover first and a science writer second. It's a very personal book, yes, an angry book, written because I feel very passionate about Félicette's story and about getting it "out there" into the world. Not just to even things up and make people aware that animal space flights didn't begin and end with Laika but also, I suppose, if I'm being truly honest, as a kind of apology to Félicette for what happened to her.

I'm sure that at the time the people involved in Félicette's mission felt justified doing what they were doing. It really was a different time, a different age. The whole world had gone Space Crazy after Sputnik, Laika, Gagarin and Shepard, and everyone was so bedazzled by the promise of space travel, so hypnotised by the excitement, glamour and romance of it that they rushed headlong towards that Final Frontier like zombies pushing at a wire fence, and they did things that they shouldn't have done.

We know now that Félicette's flight had little if any impact on the space program as a whole, and on French plans to put people into space specifically. Some would say that her death was totally in vain, her life wasted, and I'd be one of them. But it's true, hindsight *is* always 20/20, and without a TARDIS or some other time machine to use to go back to 1963 and change history there's nothing we can do. All we can do is tell Félicette's story, share it with others, and make sure she isn't ignored or forgotten. We owe her so much more, but if that's all we can do then we should. We must.

And that's what I've tried to do with this book. So, thank you for reading it (hopefully after buying it!) and for letting me pull up a chair at your table and tell you Félicette's story. Now go and give your cat (or dog, or whatever special animal you share your life with) an extra-long hug. And the next time you find yourself out under a clear, starry sky, look up, pick a star – any star, it really doesn't matter which one – and think of Félicette, the cat that went into space.

Thank you.

Stuart Atkinson

Kendal, Cumbria, April 2022

Félicette

ACKNOWLEDGEMENTS

I had a lot of help – directly and indirectly – putting this book together. I'd like to say thank you to the following people who either helped make it happen, or inspired me to start writing it:

Stella Coxon, my hugely supportive partner who always gives me the time I need to research and write. I couldn't do any of this without her.

Matthew Serge Guy, for his determination to honour Félicette's memory, and ensure her story is known, by crowd-funding the design and construction of a statue of her, which is now on display at the International Space University in Strasbourg

Gill Parker, who sculpted the beautiful statue of Félicette, and very generously sent me photos of the statue being designed and cast. www.gillparker.com

Patrick Roberts, the webmaster (is that still a title in 2020?) of the fantastic "Pure n Furr" website, www.purr-n-furr.org.uk on which I found a lot of information about Félicette and other cats mentioned in this book. The website stopped being updated in January 2019 but is an absolute treasure trove of information about famous cats, cats from history, cats in entertainment and elsewhere. Just go to the website and you'll see what I mean – but be prepared to lose the next several hours because once you start browsing it you'll have a hard time pulling yourself away..!

Kerrie Dougherty, Australian space expert who very kindly sent me a copy of the paper she co-authored about Félicette and many useful photos too.

Philippe Junge, one of the aforementioned paper's co-authors, who very kindly answered questions for me.

Raphael Roettgen, CFA, who very kindly sent me some photos he took at the unveiling ceremony for Félicette's statue at the ISU

Geraldine Moser, who also very kindly sent me some photos of the Félicette statue at the ISU

Monika Landy-Gyebnar, long time Facebook friend who has always been very supportive of my writing and supported this book by taking and sending me pictures of a neighbourhood cat that looks spookily like Félicette!

Kimberlie Hamilton, friend and author of several books about amazing animals including *Rebel Cats – Brave Tales of Feisty Felines*, who has been very supportive of my efforts to make Félicette's story better known.

And of course…

Jess, our beautiful/mad rescue cat, who has managed to calm me down and stop me getting too angry and depressed while writing this by jumping up onto my lap and melting on me like a Salvador Dali clock, giving me all the love and affection that, sadly, Félicette never had a chance to give to anyone.

ABOUT THE AUTHOR

I am a writer and amateur astronomer living in Kendal (as in the Mint Cake, floods and traffic jams, yes...!) and I have been writing astronomy books for children since 1988, when my first title – *Journey Into Space*- was published by Viking-Kestrel, with a foreword by famous science fiction author Isaac Asimov.

I have now had a total of 12 children's astronomy reference books published, including *A Cat's Guide to The Night Sky* which was published by Laurence King in October 2019. Since its publication the book has been translated into 20 languages worldwide, has won a major award in Germany (the EMYS children's non-fiction prize), was longlisted for the 2019 SLA Information Book Award and has been featured and enthusiastically reviewed on many blogs and websites. I have attended various literary festivals and organised author events in bookshops, libraries and museums promoting the book. My latest book was *The Solar System – A Ladybird Book* – which was published by Ladybird last summer.

For the past 25 years I have been an astronomy and "space" editor/consultant for many publishers, including Ladybird, Raintree, Templar, Buster and Walker Books, where I worked as consultant on their multi-award winning *Curiosity: The Story of a Mars Rover book*, written by Markus Motum. Most recently I have been the fact checker/consultant for two books written by popular Sky at Night presenter Dr Maggie Ader-in-Pocock for Buster books.

Since 1994 I have also edited or acted as a consultant/expert on almost every astronomy- and space-related title published by Usborne Publishing. I was consultant on the award-winning *The Story of Astronomy and Space* and *The Astronauts Handbook*, which was produced in co-operation with the European Space Agency with input from British astronaut Tim Peake.

I have also written for many of the major monthly astronomy magazines, and now write regularly for **BBC Sky at Night** magazine and ***All About Space*** magazine.

In addition to doing all this writing about astronomy and space, I am also very busy in the field of science Education and Outreach. I regularly give talks about astronomy and space exploration in schools and to community groups. I also broadcast regularly on my local BBC station, BBC Radio Cumbria. For several years now I have been the Comet Section Director for the Society for Popular Astronomy, and write for their website and Facebook page.

Oh, and I write astronomical poetry too! My "astro-poems" have been featured on the websites of several NASA missions, and are even displayed on the walls at NASA's Jet Propulsion Laboratory in California.

You can find more information about all of the above on my website:

www.stuartatkinson.wordpress.com

Having said all that, writing is not my full-time occupation! I am a Support Worker in a busy residential care home for the elderly – quite a contrast to my other life as an author and all-round space cadet, as you can imagine…

Stuart Atkinson

Twitter (X): @mars_stu
Facebook: www.facebook.com/stuartatk
Website: www.stuartatkinson.wordpress.com

ILLUSTRATION NOTES

Cover: artwork by the author, based on the well-known "postcard of participation" produced after Felicette's flight

P8: space cats "line up" image generously provided by Purr-n-Fur's Patrick Roberts

P23: Felicette portrait processed from a screengrab of YouTube video

P47: Felicette statue under construction, generously provided by the sculptor, Gill Parker.

P48: Felicette statue after unveiling, generously provided by Philippe Jung

P60: artwork created by author

P67: artwork created by author

P74: artwork created by author

P79: artwork created by author

P89: sketch by Louie Stowell, author of the best-selling "Loki" books

P93: photo of myself and Jess, taken by Stella Coxon

BOOKS

I'm recommending these books because they either helped me directly with researching facts, figures and dates, or they inspired and encouraged me simply by featuring Félicette:

Animals in Space
by Colin Burgess and Chris Dubbs (Springer Praxis)

Rebel Cats – Brave Tales of Feisty Felines
by Kimberlie Hamilton

Printed in Great Britain
by Amazon